The Frozen-Water Trade

The Frozen-Water Trade

A TRUE STORY

GAVIN WEIGHTMAN

NEW YORK

Library of Congress Cataloging-in-Publication Data

Weightman, Gavin.
    The frozen-water trade / Gavin Weightman.—1st ed.
      p. cm.
    Includes index.
    ISBN-13 978-0-7868-8640-1
    1. Ice industry—North America—History. I. Title.

  HD9481.N72 W44 2002
  380.1'427—dc21

                       2001039803

FIRST EDITION

10 9 8 7 6 5 4 3 2 1

In fond memory of my uncle
Morris Weightman

Contents

List of Illustrations

Frederic Tudor. (*From* Old Boston Days and Ways; *reproduced courtesy of the Bostonian Society/Old State House*)

The first entry in Tudor's Ice House Diary, on August 5, 1805. (*The Tudor Ice Co. Collection, Vol. 13. Baker Library, Harvard Business School*)

The cover of Tudor's first diary. (*The Tudor Ice Co. Collection, Vol. 13. Baker Library, Harvard Business School*)

Design for the kind of icehouse built in Europe and America in the early nineteenth century. (*Mary Evans Picture Library*)

An 1845 advertisement for the Fresh Pond Hotel in Cambridge, Massachusetts. (*Cambridge Historical Society Collection, Cambridge Historical Commission*)

Ice harvesters at work on Fresh Pond, 1830. (*From* Ballou's Pictorial; *reproduced courtesy of the Rare Books Department, Boston Public Library*)

Ice tools. (*Courtesy of Maine Maritime Museum, Bath, Maine*)

Ploughing and storing ice on the Hudson River. (*Mary Evans Picture Library*)

An 1841 map of Fresh Pond, showing each merchant's share of the ice crop. (*Rare Books Department, Boston Public Library*)

Acknowledgments

The single greatest pleasure I had in researching the ice trade was the time I spent in Boston, Frederic Tudor's hometown. His diaries, his Calcutta Book, and much of his correspondence is held in the beautiful Baker Library at Harvard Business School, and I would like to thank the staff for their help in finding documents for me and allowing me desk space in their small reading room. It was a thrill to read sections of the diaries, but also quite daunting, for it would take so long to study them all. The only biography of Tudor that made use of the diaries had been published in the 1930s in the *Proceedings of the Massachusetts Historical Society*. It was while I was working there that I learned that a much fuller account of the Tudor family had been in preparation by Carl Seaburg and Stanley Paterson. Both elderly gentlemen had sadly died before they found a publisher. However, Carl's brother Alan Seaburg had taken on the task of editing the text with a view to publication by the Massachusetts Historical Society, and he very kindly allowed me to read it, bringing the manuscript with him on one of his regular trips to London. I owe him a very special thanks. As well as putting me in touch with Alan Seaburg, the staff at the Massachusetts Historical Society unearthed much valuable material.

Aurore Eaton of the Cambridge Historical Society found for me a number of articles that included Benjamin Waterhouse's wonderful description of the wagons carrying Tudor's ice from Fresh Pond to Charlestown Harbor in the 1830s. Many thanks to her and the gentleman who went through the Society's archives for me. Although we were unable to meet up, Philip Chadwick Foster Smith— "Chad" to his friends—author of the charming monograph about Wenham Lake, *Crystal Blocks of Yankee Coldness*, gave me a great deal of help and generously sent me a photocopy of a letter written by Frederic's brother William at the time the two first began the ice trade. Chad had bought it from a bookseller, and it was in none of the libraries or collections.

I found David G. Dickason's study of the Boston-India ice trade very valuable, and Philip C. Whitney of Fitchburg, who still demonstrates each winter the use of the horse-drawn ice cutter, gave me a vivid description of how it is done.

The Peabody Museum in Salem gave me the story of the miraculous reappearance in America of the cup presented to one of Frederic's partners by Lord Bentinck, Governor General of Bengal, in commemoration of the first delivery of Boston ice to Calcutta. The Bostonian Society unearthed for me several valuable books and articles, as did the Cambridge Historical Buildings Commission. Nathan Lipfert at Maine Maritime Museum pointed me in the direction of a copy of Jenny Everson's charming book *The Tidewater*

Ice of the Kennebec River. I bought it on the Internet via Barnes & Noble's out-of-print-books page.

In London the British Library was, as always, a gold mine. Here I could track down an astonishing range of material, from the *New Englands Farmers' Weekly* of the 1820s to the *Calcutta Courier* and other Bengal newspapers published in the 1830s and held in the India section. Simon Blundell, the librarian at The Reform Club in London, found for me a number of valuable books and nineteenth-century issues of *Punch*. The London Library proved invaluable as always. Kate Simpson researched the New York newspapers from the 1870s until the early 1900s with diligence and presented me with a superb set of photocopies of issues that headlined the "ice famines" and corruption stories of the period. My friend Brian Stewart at CBC in Canada also found some very useful archival material, and he and Tina Strebotjnac provided a helpful critique of an early draft of the book.

I would like to thank John Keay for his very perceptive comments, Charles Walker at Peters, Fraser and Dunlop for his encouragement and interest, Richard Johnson for his enthusiastic reception of the book, and Robert Lacey for his meticulous and very thoughtful work as editor. Caroline Hotblack gave tremendous help with the illustrations. Thanks, too, to Vanessa Frances for providing me with such a pleasant place to stay in Boston.

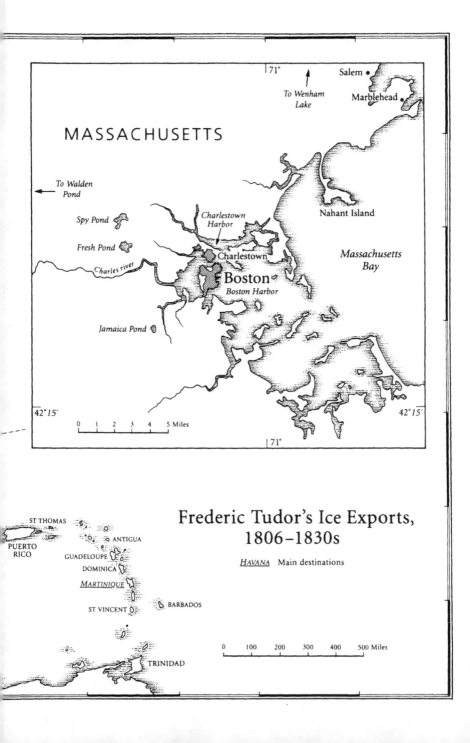

MASSACHUSETTS

To Wenham
Lake

71°

Salem •

Marblehead •

To Walden
Pond

Spy Pond

Fresh Pond

Charles river

Charlestown
Harbor

Charlestown

Boston

Boston Harbor

Nahant Island

Massachusetts
Bay

Jamaica Pond

42°15′

0   1   2   3   4   5 Miles

42°15′

71°

ST THOMAS

PUERTO
RICO

GUADELOUPE

DOMINICA

MARTINIQUE

ST VINCENT

ANTIGUA

BARBADOS

TRINIDAD

Frederic Tudor's Ice Exports,
1806–1830s

HAVANA Main destinations

0   100   200   300   400   500 Miles

Introduction

The inspiration for this book was one of those scraps of information that lodge in the mind and refuse to go away. I had read somewhere, while researching the history of nineteenth-century London, that Queen Victoria had for a time enjoyed a supply of ice from Massachusetts. It was delivered by an American enterprise called the Wenham Lake Ice Company, which in the 1840s had an ice store and a shop in London with a window onto The Strand, in which a large cube of crystal-clear ice about two feet square was displayed every day in the summer. Sometimes a colorful New England fish called a "pickerel" would be frozen into the block of ice on show.

I wondered if the ingenious Americans, pioneers of mass production, great inventors and modernizers, had stolen a march on the rest of the world and devised a form of refrigeration that could produce ice cheaply enough to sell at a price the wealthy in London could afford. I discovered that there was, in fact, a huge ice industry in nineteenth-century North America, but that it was not at all what I had imagined.

Ice became essential to the American way of life from the mid-nineteenth century. Americans made ice cream at home on Sundays, had iceboxes in which to keep butter and milk fresh, were served iced drinks in hotels, and were dependent on ice for the preservation of fresh food long before there was any artificial refrigeration. All the ice was natural, cut from lakes and rivers in the winter, stored in huge icehouses, and delivered to customers in horse-drawn wagons. A great quantity was exported in the holds of sailing ships: that is how the ice from Wenham Lake, near Salem, Massachusetts, was carried to London. In fact, the New England ice trade had begun not as a domestic business but with exports to the West Indies, and it had achieved a much more remarkable feat before any ice was sold in London: in the 1830s, Boston merchants began selling ice to the British community in Calcutta. The voyage to India was about 16,000 miles, and under favorable conditions took about 130 days. Yet for fifty years the sale of New England ice to Calcutta was a profitable business. In fact, its success saved from financial catastrophe the man who had first dreamed up the ice trade.

He was Frederic Tudor, surely one of most remarkable businessmen of the nineteenth century. Tudor was a diminutive, pigheaded Bostonian who dedicated most of his working life to supplying ice to the tropics. He suffered the humiliation of bankruptcy, was jailed for debt, endured a mental breakdown, but came through it all to father six children after the age of fifty and to die in 1864, at age eighty, a wealthy man with a country estate. At no time did Tudor, or any of those who became his competitors in the ice business, make use of artificial refrigeration. With one or two trivial exceptions, all the ice marketed in Tudor's lifetime was "harvested" from lakes and rivers that froze in the winter. In the holds of ships, the ice was preserved through many days, and even weeks, sailing through tropical heat, insulated by the sawdust supplied by timber mills in Maine.

The ice trade was carried on in a century of great inventions—the electric telegraph, railways, steam-driven machines of all kinds, and gas and electric light. It continued long after Tudor's death, into the age of gas engines and electric trams. As late as 1907, New York, by then the quintessential modern city of skyscrapers and motorcars, was absolutely reliant on natural ice harvested from lakes and rivers, including the Hudson, and on imports of Kennebec River ice sent by ship from Maine. When winter weather was mild, the *New York Times* would warn of an ice "famine" the following summer, and every year newspaper articles would appear promising an end to the reliance on harvested ice.

Frederic Tudor had not anticipated that the trade he began would lead to such ice addiction among his fellow Americans. From the time he first shipped lake ice to the West Indies in 1806 to the beginnings of the Calcutta trade in the 1830s, he clung to one conviction: people living in tropical climates would pay a good price for ice if they could get it. The inhabitants of Havana, Cuba, and the British sweltering in Calcutta could make ice cream, cool their drinks, and relieve their suffering from fevers with ice harvested from the clear waters of New England's many spring-fed ponds. They could even enjoy crisp

Baldwin apples from the orchards of Massachusetts, and fresh-churned butter, which Tudor packed in barrels and stowed alongside the ice.

The techniques Tudor and his employees developed for cutting, storing, and shipping ice were in time adopted across all the areas of North America where winters were hard enough to produce a salable crop. Ice was shipped down the eastern seaboard and carried across the continent in insulated railroad cars to satisfy the ever-growing demands of the first nation in history to enjoy refrigeration not as a luxury for the rich, but as an everyday necessity for a very wide section of its population.

There had been earlier ice trades. In the sixteenth century, the mountain ranges that surround the Mediterranean and are high enough to remain snow-capped in summer provided refrigeration for those living on the torrid coasts. Snow and ice gathered on the upper slopes of the mountains were packed in straw baskets and brought down the winding Alpine tracks on donkeys. A similar trade had existed in South America for centuries, and continues in some places to this day. Wherever there were accessible mountains that carried summer snow, and towns close enough to provide a market for it, there was likely to be an ice trade. But the American industry was on a much larger scale, and was far more sophisticated than anything before it.

The harvest, which lasted for a few weeks, usually between January and March, took place across that huge region of North America where the winters are hard enough to freeze lakes and rivers solid. Whether it was on the Hudson River, one of the New England ponds, the Kennebec River in Maine, or in the

Midwest, it presented the same extraordinary winter tableau, and in many places drew crowds of spectators.

After a week or so of subzero temperatures, soundings would be taken to check the thickness of the ice. If it had frozen to a depth of eighteen inches or more, it was ready—strong enough to support the weight of hundreds of men and horses, and thick enough to yield good-sized cubes of ice.

Migrant workers who lodged close to the frozen lakes and rivers joined local farmworkers to make up teams of ice harvesters. Blacksmiths shod the heavy horses with spiked shoes. The men wore boots with cork soles so they could get a grip on the ice, and wrapped their legs in layers of cloth to protect them from the cold. All the while, they watched the weather: a warm spell could quickly ruin the ice, while a fall of snow might delay the cutting, for the ice would have to be cleared with horse-drawn scrapers before its surface could be marked out. Often they worked at night, by torchlight. Ice was valuable, and competing ice companies working on the same lake or river had to observe boundaries: ownership was established by buying sections of shoreline on which huge timber ice stores were built.

Once a favorable area of ice was established and the snow cleared to reveal the crystal surface of the ice, it could be marked out. This was generally the work of men who steered iron cutters drawn by teams of two horses across the surface, creating parallel lines in one direction and then, working at right angles to the first cuts, another set of parallel lines, so that the whole area to be cut was divided up into regular squares. The favored size of the cubes varied according to the market for which the ice was destined. Blocks for India or the West Indies were the largest, those destined for American cities often smaller—a "New York" ice cube was twenty-two inches square.

When the surface was marked out, horse-drawn plows with metal teeth cut far enough down into the first grooves to enable men with long-handled chisels to prise the blocks free. The giant ice cubes were then coaxed along channels of free water to a mechanism that hoisted them into the timber icehouse. Loading was from the top, the blocks sliding down a chute from which they were hauled into regular stacks, like huge building blocks. Sawdust was put between and around the blocks as insulation. Stacked like that while awaiting shipment, the ice cubes were able to survive for several years, shrinking slowly through each summer and refreezing in winter.

Before the building of railroads to transport it, ice was carried from the stores to a port or nearby town in wagons drawn by teams of horses or oxen. From there, most of it was moved by ship, and could not be carried until the spring thaw. On the Hudson, specially designed barges carried the ice down to New York. In city centers, huge ice warehouses provided depots from which ice was distributed to customers. In the home, Americans kept blocks of ice cut to a standard size in what were called "refrigerators," or "iceboxes"—there are people living in rural areas who still remember these very well. It took a number of years to perfect the design of these containers for storing ice, for this proved to be technically difficult. Refrigerators were chiefly built of wood and lined with metal, with different compartments for keeping food fresh. Those who could afford it had a fresh block of ice delivered daily, for which they paid a weekly or monthly subscription.

American ice was crystal clear, and considered clean enough to put directly into drinks, a custom that in the nineteenth century was novel to Europeans. Before the Civil War of the 1860s, the mint juleps of New Orleans, and other southern cocktails, were made with ice shipped down from Boston, and the abundance of natural ice that could be delivered daily made it possible for Americans to enjoy homemade ice cream right through the summer. This required an additional piece of equipment, for it is impossible to freeze liquids simply by immersing them in ice; a bit of alchemy is required. It had been discovered centuries earlier, possibly in China, that a mixture of salt and ice will draw heat from a metal container immersed in it and will reduce the temperature inside it to below zero. If a liquid is put into the container, it will freeze solid. To make ice cream with a pleasing, light texture, it is important to stir the cream as it freezes. Nineteenth-century ice cream–making machines therefore included a paddle mechanism to stir the mixture as it solidified.

Frederic Tudor, promoting his pioneer shipment of ice to the West Indies in 1806, can be credited with being the first person to sell ice cream in that part of the world. The use of salt and ice to make a "freezing mixture" was really the only bit of science or chemistry Tudor ever employed in the ice business. All the other innovations to do with the cutting and storing of natural ice—and there were a great many of them—were arrived at by trial and error and close observation of the keeping properties of frozen water. Whereas heat could easily be produced by the burning of fuels such as coal, the reverse process of generating low temperatures was much more complex. Even today, when half the population of the world enjoys the benefits of domestic refrigeration, very few people understand how the cooler or the ice-making machine works. It was not until the end of the nineteenth century that the physics of heat was properly understood, and even then there were technical problems with making machines that could produce artificial ice cheaply enough to compete with the abundant natural supplies from frozen lakes and rivers. The modern domestic refrigerator is powered by electricity, which was not widely available in homes until the 1920s. The first successful artificial refrigerators were large industrial plants that required enormous power. The ice they produced was delivered to customers who made use of it in exactly the same way as they did supplies of natural ice—by placing it in their iceboxes.

It was in places where the supply of natural ice presented special problems that artificially manufactured ice was first used on any scale. As early as the 1860s, the southern states of America began to depend on artificial ice when shipments of lake and river ice from the north ceased during the Civil War. Calcutta got its first artificial ice plants around 1880, putting an end to the Boston trade. But in most of North America, natural-ice harvesting gained ground continuously in the nineteenth century and did not become established in many regions until after the 1880s. The boom in Maine came in the last decades of the century when New York, Baltimore, Philadelphia, and Washington were desperate for supplies.

When the first comprehensive report on the ice industry of the United States was commissioned in 1879 as part of a national census, it was estimated that about eight million tons were harvested annually, though the business was so extensive and production so poorly documented that this was, at best, a well-informed guess. The figures were put together by one Henry Hall, who signed himself "special agent" and gave an account of the great growth of the industry in the preceding ten years. Of the eight million tons of ice harvested, about five million reached the consumer—the rest melted during shipment and storage. By far the biggest market was in New York, and none of its ice was manufactured artificially: it was all cut in winter and stored in hundreds of timber warehouses that lined the lakes and rivers and had a capacity of up to fifty thousand tons each. Between New York and Albany, 150 miles up the Hudson River, there were 135 icehouses, but even this was not enough to supply the metropolis, which relied heavily on imports. In fact, in the year of the great ice census, New York and Philadelphia suffered one of their recurrent ice "famines," when unseasonably warm weather destroyed the harvest on the Hudson and local lakes, and the price of ice rose from $4 to $5 a ton. That year the ice was fifteen to twenty inches thick in Maine, a top-quality crop, and it could be shipped down to New York at an estimated cost of $1.50 a ton. This produced a frenzy of harvesting on the Kennebec, Penobscot, and Sheepscot Rivers, and two thousand cargoes of ice packed in hay and sawdust were shipped south to New York, Philadelphia, and other more southern cities, where they were sold for a total of around $1.5 million.

Though the demand for ice rose annually, the New York suppliers did not explore the use of artificial refrigeration. Instead, they began to buy up sections of the Kennebec River shoreline and to erect great wooden warehouses there, transforming the landscape of the river for many miles. It was the same farther inland, where ice companies bought up shoreline along the lakes and put up storehouses to supply the meat industry of Chicago and the brewers of Milwaukee, as well as millions of domestic consumers.

The first real crisis in the natural-ice trade was caused not by competition from artificial manufacture, but by pollution. As the cities grew, they encroached on the rivers and lakes from which the ice was cut, and soon there were health scares. The authorities reported that the Hudson River was becoming an open sewer, yet ice cut from it ended up in drinks served in New York hotels and put into domestic refrigerators. This produced a search for cleaner supplies away from towns, and stimulated the search for a means of manufacturing ice with pure water. The realization that the bacteria that cause diseases such as typhoid were not killed off in frozen water added to the urgency of finding safer forms of refrigeration.

The natural-ice trade began to decline from the early decades of the twentieth century, though in more remote areas of North America where electric power was not available but lake ice was abundant in winter, it survived as late as the 1950s. As ice harvesting died out, the evidence of its former vast scale rapidly disappeared. There was no alternative use for the great icehouses, many of which simply burned down, often set alight by a spark from a steam train—they were surprisingly flammable, as most were made of wood and kept as dry as possible to better preserve the blocks of ice they housed. But the majority were demolished or simply rotted away.

Over a wide area of the northern states, young diving enthusiasts with no knowledge of the former ice trade still emerge from lakes and rivers clutching an impressive variety of odd implements—plows and chisels and scrapers that fell through the ice during the harvesting. One or two museums keep small displays of these tools, and collectors have preserved manufacturers' catalogs that proudly present their versions of the ice plow, the ice saw, the grapple, the Jack grapple, the breaking-off bar, the caulk bar, the packing chisel, the house bar, the fork bar, the float hook, the line marker, and many other specialist implements the use of which has long been forgotten.

The inner-city icehouses have also gone, and the ice wagon and the iceman are rapidly fading memories (although the latter survived for a time in countless bawdy jokes and in the title of Eugene O'Neill's play *The Iceman Cometh*). All that is left in America of this once-great industry is the water itself, which provided a continuously renewable supply of ice each winter. There are few memorials on the banks of the rivers and lakes that once produced such a vital crop, although a small museum close to Wenham Lake, near Salem, Massachusetts, has some souvenirs and a colorful account of the area's part in the ice trade.

Most of the few histories of the ice trade are local publications, for despite the industry's extent, it was, like farming or the mining of coal, of greatest interest to those communities that earned their living from it and whose families retain some memories passed down from earlier generations. The shipping of ice over hundreds and even thousands of miles became so routine that few records remain in the memoirs of sea captains or sailors, who generally treated the blocks as just another cargo, like sugar or wheat. Even the epic voyages from Boston to Calcutta appear to have left little impression on the elite crews who carried ice and who sometimes called the business, in their matter-of-fact seafaring fashion, the "frozen-water trade."

I have borrowed the seaman's term for the business as the title of this book. It struck me when I first came across it as evocative of an industry that grew so impressively in the nineteenth century without any recourse to modern inventions. Its success was grounded in human qualities and skills that have been neglected as driving forces in an age now characterized in history books by the novelties and excitements of electricity and steam. Timber, sailcloth, horsepower, manpower, and the traditional skills of blacksmiths, farmers, and sailors made America the first-ever refrigerated nation. This is the story of how that was achieved.

1

The Frozen Assets of New England

When the brothers William and Frederic Tudor agreed to put together what money they had in the summer of 1805 and invest it in a scheme to sell ice to the West Indies, they held the plan close to their chests. They had dreamed up the idea after spending some pleasant weeks on the family farm, Rockwood, near Boston. It was just a few miles inland from this city, the great port that seethed with shipping and merchants, many of whom had made fortunes trading around the world in all kinds of luxury goods. New England itself had little of value to export: there was no iron or coal or cotton, and the farmland was picturesque but poor. Most of Boston's trade was secondhand: the Yankee merchants had a sharp eye for other nations' goods, which they bought and sold as their ships scoured the world for bargains.

Just to the north, the port of Salem had more or less cornered the market in peppercorns, reexporting in 1805 7.5 million tons of the spice, which was greatly valued as a food preservative in the days before refrigeration. And in 1783, the year the younger Tudor brother Frederic was born, a syndicate of Boston merchants had made a fortune from a shipload of ginseng that they sold in Canton. The herbal root, rare in China, where it was greatly prized as an aphrodisiac and a tonic, had been found growing in abundance in North America, and the first Boston cargo was said to equal ten times the annual Chinese consumption. But even the shrewd merchants of Massachusetts had failed to realize that each winter a local product of dazzlingly high quality was left to dissolve away each spring, while in the tropical islands of the West Indies and the plantation states of southern America it would be worth its weight in gold. That, at any rate, was how the Tudor brothers saw it, and why they wanted to keep their scheme for selling ice in tropical climates a secret. Once Boston merchants got wind of their brilliant plan, they would face stiff competition.

The elder brother, William, who was twenty-six years old and a Harvard graduate with some worldly experience after traveling in Europe, was just a bit skeptical once he had considered the practical problems of the venture. But Frederic, not quite twenty-two and the maverick of the distinguished Boston family, was convinced it would make them a fortune, and that within a few years they would be, as he put it, "inevitably and unavoidably rich." As it turned out, Frederic did make his fortune selling ice, but there was nothing inevitable or unavoidable about his eventual success. The fact that he prospered at all, after suffering years of ridicule and hardship, was more of a miracle than something preordained. Then, as now, the notion that it was possible to cut lake ice in winter in New England and sell it the following summer 1,500 miles away in Cuba or Martinique, with no artificial refrigeration to prevent it from melting, was thought to be ridiculous.

Nevertheless, the plan did make some sense. The Tudor family was privileged. The brothers' grandfather Deacon Tudor was a self-made baker and merchant who had sailed from Devon, England, in 1715, at the age of six. His mother was a young widow who had remarried in America, well enough for John to receive a basic education. John did sufficiently well in business to send his youngest son, William, to Harvard to study law. He also bought the hundred-acre farm, Rockwood, as a kind of rugged country estate where the family could spend the hot summer months away from their town house in Boston. At Rockwood, like a few of the better-off Bostonians, the Tudors had an icehouse that was stocked in winter from a pond on the farm that usually froze solid in January and February. As children, Frederic and his brothers and sisters* enjoyed ice cream in the summer and took their drinks cooled with chunks of crystal-clear ice from Rockwood Pond. This was a great luxury. In Europe, icehouses—traditionally underground and lined with brick or stone—had long been a privilege of the wealthy, who could afford to excavate them on their estates and had the

---

*Six children survived infancy: William (born in 1779), John Henry (born in 1782), Frederic (born in 1783), Emma Jane (born in 1785), Delia (born in 1787), and Henry James, known as Harry (born in 1791).

manpower to fill them in winter with ice from their frozen ornamental lakes.

This luxury was denied to those who lived in tropical climates, including the colonial rulers of the West Indian islands and the prosperous plantation owners of the cotton belt in South Carolina, Georgia, and Louisiana. What would they pay for a shipload of perspiring New England ice during their most torrid season, when the heat was hardly bearable and yellow fever raged? Selling them ice, it seemed to Frederic Tudor, would be an excellent and simple proposition provided a few technicalities could be sorted out. It was a straightforward matter of supply and demand, once the problem had been solved of how to keep the supply from melting before it reached the demand.

The Tudor brothers were in the happy position of having a bit of family money to invest. In 1794, when Frederic was eleven, their grandfather John had died at the age of eighty-six, and had left everything to their father, William. This small fortune consisted of forty thousand dollars in cash and investments, some properties in Boston, and Rockwood. William was always known affectionately in the family as "the Judge," a title he had acquired when he served as judge advocate* in George Washington's army. His Harvard education and his military service afforded him many good connections in New England society, where he was well liked for his jovial personality. Before 1794, he had practiced as a lawyer, but he felt he was well enough off

---

*A military officer with legal training who acts as prosecutor at courts-martial and gives advice on legal matters to the officers sitting as judge and jury.

after John died to give up work and live the life of a landed gentleman. The Judge was a generous man and a spendthrift, and the family lived well. He could afford to send his sons to Harvard and to give them a generous allowance that enabled them to travel, and sometimes to dabble in speculation.

In preparation for Harvard, Frederic was sent to Boston Latin School. At the age of thirteen, he decided that college was a waste of time, dropped out of school, and took a job as an apprentice in a Boston store. His mother, Delia, a cultured woman who was anxious that her sons be properly educated, did not approve. Nor did his eldest brother, William. But neither had any authority over him, and at the time Frederic left school, the Judge was off on a jaunt to Europe. Frederic wrote to him: "I hope you will not be displeased with my going so young." When the Judge returned to Boston, Frederic had already given up his apprenticeship and was spending his days on the Rockwood farm, hunting and fishing with a black servant of the family who had been given the name Sambo. Frederic loved Rockwood and sometimes imagined he could make the farm pay, but he spent most of his time on little schemes that came to nothing, such as designing a water pump that he believed would make ships unsinkable.

When he was seventeen years old and still hanging idly around Rockwood, an opportunity arose that would have an influence on Frederic's later conviction that there would be a demand for ice in the West Indies. His nineteen-year-old brother, John Henry, had a bad knee that had turned him into an invalid. Anxious about his son's health, the Judge suggested that Frederic take John away somewhere. The boys were enthusiastic, and chose to go to Havana, then a thriving trading port on the Spanish island of Cuba. It would not be just a convalescent trip: while they were there they might try their hand at trading in coffee or sugar—they had already made a small profit selling mahogany furniture to Havana. On February 26, 1801, they sailed from Boston on the *Patty* with $1,000 in travel money given to them by their father.

John Henry left a jaundiced account of the voyage. Both brothers were seasick for the first week or so, got sunburned, and hated the shipboard diet of beef and soup. They were at sea for a month, arriving in Havana at the end of March. At first they thought Cuba a kind of paradise, full of excitement and tropical fruit, and for two months they took tours, engaged in a little trade, and lost money. But by the end of May, as Havana heated up and the mosquitoes and scorpions became bothersome, they decided to leave. John Henry's knee was getting worse, and gave him pain every day. At the beginning of June, they bought passage on a ship bound for Charleston, South Carolina, loaded with molasses, which gave off a fierce and heavy stench. To ensure that they would eat tolerably well on this voyage, the brothers loaded up for their own consumption 192 eggs, which would be enough for half a dozen or more each a day.

In Charleston, they were entertained by some kindly Bostonians who were living there, but the heat was just as bad as in Havana. The brothers sailed on to Virginia, driven north by the rising summer temperatures, and, still with their "tongues hanging out," as John Henry put it, cruised into the Potomac River, where they had a glimpse of Mount Vernon, which had been George Washington's estate. In search of a cure for John Henry, they went on overland to a spa in Bath, Pennsylvania. Each day his health was deteriorating—he may have been suffering from bone tuberculosis—and lumps appeared on his side. In August, they met up by chance with their mother and eldest brother, William, and all four went to Philadelphia, from where Frederic and William took the stagecoach back to Boston. At the end of January 1802, John Henry died in Philadelphia, his mother by his bedside. When Frederic, back on the Rockwood estate, heard the news four months after he had last seen his brother, he was deeply affected.

Frederic's brother William, who had finished his studies, went off to Europe to broaden his education. The Judge found Frederic an unpaid position with a mercantile firm owned by his friends the Sullivan brothers. There he spent two years arranging shipments of pimento, nutmeg, sugar, and tea. With this experience behind him, the Judge felt confident enough to set Frederic up in business on his own, though he did not know what exactly he would trade in. The best bet at that time appeared to be speculation in real estate, for Boston was a growing city, and handsome profits had been made by those who owned land that could be built on. The Judge himself decided to put the family fortune into a venture in South Boston that was considered to be gilt-edged. A new bridge was being built to connect the town with an isolated area of land in the complex archipelago of Boston Bay. Frederic had a stake in it too, buying land for $7,640 in partnership with his brother William.

While they still mourned the death of John Henry, the family was able to look forward to a happy event, the marriage of Frederic's younger sister Emma Jane. She was by all accounts an attractive young woman, and her family's wealth appeared to be assured. Her suitor was a shy young man named Robert Hallowell Gardiner, who had come into a fortune by chance. His father, Robert Hallowell, had been collector of taxes for the port of Boston before the War of Independence, and had fled to England in 1776. Robert was born in Bristol in 1782, and his family moved back to Boston the same year. When he was six years old, his maternal grandfather, Dr. Silvester Gardiner, who owned a very large estate on the Kennebec River, in Maine, died, leaving everything to Robert's uncle William. A year later, William died and left everything to Robert, provided he agreed to change his name to Gardiner. He would come into his inheritance on his twenty-second birthday.

Robert had studied at Harvard, and when he first met Emma Tudor, he was a member of the New England elite, a very eligible young man. His marriage to Emma was a great match for the Tudors, and would turn out to be vital for the new trade Frederic and William were about to embark upon. Though they fell out in later life, Robert Gardiner would be the very best friend and supporter Frederic could have hoped for in the years ahead. It was in the heady atmosphere of the summer of 1805, when the wedding was celebrated with picnics and parties on the Tudors' Rockwood estate, that Frederic and William finally decided to embark on the venture they had talked about for some time.

Emma had married Robert on June 25, 1805. A few weeks later, Frederic bought a leather-bound farmer's almanac and inscribed on the cover the title "Ice House Diary," above a crude drawing of the kind of icehouse, if not the very one, the family had at Rockwood. He also wrote the inscription "He who gives back at the first repulse and without striking the second blow, despairs of success, has never been, is not, and never will be, a hero in love, war or business." It is probable he added that later, inscribing it as if in stone on the illustration of the ice-house, for he had absolutely no idea in 1805 of the trials he was to face over the next ten years.

The first entry in the diary, written in Frederic's spidery hand, reads: "Plan etc for transporting Ice to Tropical Climates. Boston Augst 1st 1805 William and myself have this day determined to get together what property we have and embark in the undertaking of carrying ice to the West Indies the ensuing winter." There is a note written later to the effect that William was not very enthusiastic, and had to be persuaded that it was worth giving the venture a try.

A Tudor family legend had it that it was, in the first place, William's idea. It would have been typical of him, as he was full of hare-brained schemes that came to nothing, and in his privately published autobiography, *Early Recollections,* Robert Gardiner remembered William, at a picnic, suggesting selling ice to the West Indies. To the end of his life, Frederic disputed this, and maintained that it was his inspiration. Whatever the truth of the matter, it was without doubt Frederic who took the idea seriously, and who dedicated his life to making it work.

The second entry in the diary is for August 12. Frederic writes that he is off on a trip with his cousin James Savage to visit Niagara Falls, and expects to return in October. In the meantime, he and William had been laying plans for the shipment of ice that winter. They had realized they would need substantial financial backing, and hoped they might be able to persuade the U.S. Congress to grant them a monopoly in the trade, for once everyone in Boston saw how profitable the shipping of ice was, there would be immediate and damaging competition.

Puffed up with youthful enthusiasm and naïveté, Frederic could not imagine that such a brilliant scheme could fail to make him and his brother a fortune. His excitement leaps from the pages of his diary as he drafts a letter to a business associate of his father, Harrison Gray Otis, a distinguished Bostonian and U.S. senator:

> Sir, In a country where at some seasons of the year the heat is almost unsupportable, where at times the common necessary of life, water, cannot be had but in a tepid state— Ice must be considered as out doing most other luxuries.

Frederic's escape from Havana in the blazing June heat four years before with brother John Henry, only to find Charleston, South Carolina, no better, was clearly in his mind. He would have given anything for a lump of Rockwood ice when he felt the heat of Cuba that summer. But there remained the question of whether ice would last the voyage to tropical waters. Frederic had thought about this, and believed he had come across a good deal of evidence that ice could be preserved at sea. His letter to Otis continued:

> However absurd Sir the idea may at first appear that ice can be transported to tropical climates and preserved there during the most intemperate heats, yet for the fol-

lowing reasons does appear to me certain that the thing can
be done and also to a profit beyond calculation.

The evidence with which he hoped to persuade Otis to take a
stake in the business was, to say the least, patchy, and in retrospect
a little puzzling. For example, he had it on good authority that an
American sea captain had shipped ice from Norway to London
in a year when a mild winter had led to a shortage of ice in England. It is true that by the end of the eighteenth century, English
fishermen had begun using ice to preserve their catches, but there
is no record of any ice shipments from Norway to England before
1822. And even if they had been made, Frederic could have had
no idea how the ice would have been preserved onboard.

As if to prove definitively that his scheme was not absurd,
Frederic told Otis that he had also heard from a French friend
of his family that ice cream had been carried from England to
Trinidad in pots packed in earth and sand. He had also been
told—this time by a French gentleman, further evidence of his
mother's Francophile tendencies—that timber boards shipped
in winter from New England still had ice on them when they
were unloaded in the West Indies, the only instance that gentleman knew of ice being seen in that part of the world. Frederic
had also been told that it had been "experimentally proved"
that ice could be preserved in Carolina, a southern state with a
summer climate "as intemperate as most of the West Indies." He
supposed that wherever you were in the world, if you dug a hole
in the ground you would soon reach cool earth, which would
keep ice much longer than if it were left on the surface. It was
some time before he learned that this assumption was false.

Apparently Frederic knew nothing of the Mediterranean trade in Alpine ice, but he had heard of something similar in Peru, where snow from the mountains was sold in the city of Lima. All in all, Frederic was in little doubt that carrying ice to the West Indies would be pretty certain of success, and he was confident that he and his brother would make "fortunes larger than we shall know what to do with." He asked Otis, whatever his own opinion of the scheme, not to mention it to the Judge, as it was a secret and their father did "not have a hint of it."

After he had dispatched this letter, Frederic set off for Niagara Falls with his cousin James, who at that time had no idea he was to be brought in as a partner in the brothers' pioneer venture in the ice trade. James had spent most of his childhood with the Tudors and was more or less one of the family, for his mother had died when he was a boy and his father was insane and incapable of caring for him. He was the same age as Frederic, just twenty-one, and had recently graduated from Harvard. The trip to Niagara was just a youthful jaunt, but on the way, Frederic made a point of studying the construction of two icehouses he had heard about. One of them, in upstate New York, had three walls aboveground and only one cut into the earth, and Frederic was intrigued to see that it apparently kept ice as efficiently as any other icehouse. Frederic was no scientist and had absolutely no idea about the thermodynamics of icehouses, which are surprisingly complex. For most of his lifetime, the nature of heat was poorly understood. Much thought had gone into the design of icehouses both in Europe and in America, and as Frederic had suggested in his letter to Otis, it was believed that you had only to dig down a few feet anywhere in the world to find cool earth in which to store ice. In time, he realized that this was nonsense; it would prove vital for the continuation of the trade he established that ice could be preserved just as well aboveground as below, and that if the atmospheric temperature was above freezing, the only source of "cold" was the ice itself.

William, meanwhile, appears to have given the ice venture little thought, and to have spent his time enjoying the beefsteak-and-oyster dinners held weekly by members of a Boston literary society he had helped found, the Anthology Club. He had given business a try on his trip to Europe a few years earlier, and felt he had no talent or taste for it. As he did not need to earn a living, he preferred the pleasant company of Boston's young literati. It is a wonder that Frederic persuaded him to get involved in the ice trade as winter closed in on Boston in 1805. But he went along with his younger brother's plans, which were, on the face of it, quite straightforward.

European colonial powers in the West Indies each had a different set of laws and regulations relating to trade, all of them subject to rapid change as treaties were made and broken. It was the year of the Battle of Trafalgar, when Nelson won his famous victory over the combined French and Spanish fleets off the southern coast of Spain. Though the West Indies were thousands of miles away, such momentous European events sent ripples across the ocean. With its newly won independence, America was continuously adjusting its policies on trade to take into account the shifts of European power and allegiance. For reasons that were never made clear, Frederic decided the best bet for his first venture was the French island of Martinique. Maybe he feared that the most promising market, which was certainly Havana, would draw too much attention to his venture too early, or perhaps the tension between Spain and America at the time warned him off.

Wherever he sent the ice, Frederic wanted to have an officially sanctioned monopoly on the trade, for without it, he was certain prices would be driven down by competition and he would not make the profits he dreamed of. Both his brother William and his cousin James spoke French, and his mother had many friends and contacts in France, so they felt they had a good chance of presenting their case to the colonial governor, or prefect, on Martinique. The principal town on the island, St. Pierre, had a population of thirty thousand, a Tivoli pleasure garden, and sufficient perspiring expatriates to provide willing buyers of Rockwood ice.

As there was unlikely to be any ice to cut until January 1806, there was time for William and James to sail to Martinique and seek to establish exclusive rights. Once this was done, they would make some short hops to other islands that might be interested in putting in advance orders for a spring delivery of the Tudors' luxury cargo. Frederic would stay behind and make preparations for the first shipment. The whole enterprise would be funded by him, as Harrison Gray Otis had politely declined any involvement, though he thought the scheme "plausible."

As more people learned of the venture in Boston, Frederic discovered that it was not competition he had to contend with so much as ridicule. The Judge, in particular, who still believed he was going to make a killing with his South Boston land speculation, urged Frederic to abandon his crazy ice scheme.

Robert Gardiner, who was Frederic's most enthusiastic supporter, would write in his *Early Recollections*:

> The idea was considered so utterly absurd by the sober minded merchants as to be the vagary of a disordered brain, and few men would have been willing to stand the scoffs and sneers from those whose assistance it was necessary to obtain, to aid [Frederic] in his enterprise . . . Merchants were not willing to charter their vessels to carry ice. The offices declined to insure and sailors were afraid to trust themselves with such a cargo.

But Frederic was a stubborn and determined young man who seemed to thrive on the challenge of accomplishing something that others regarded as impossible and foolhardy. He fancied he cut a dashing figure around town, a dapper little man in a blue coat who was going to make a fortune from a very big and brilliant idea.

Frederic Tudor was always meticulous in keeping financial accounts. He recorded in his diary that he paid $1.50 to the boatman who rowed William and James out to the brig *Jane*, which would take them to Martinique. It was already November 2, 1805, and it would take them at least a month to reach Martinique. They would need time to deliver their letters of introduction and arrange meetings. Frederic had set his two envoys a whole range of tasks, and was anxious that they take the enterprise seriously and not consider this an excuse for a holiday. They were to arrange for gifts of ice to be offered to prominent French officials, to find an agent to handle sales, and to check out likely sites for an icehouse in St. Pierre. Most important of all, they should negotiate the privilege of a monopoly in supplying the island. As soon as they had news, they were to send Frederic a letter. This would take at least a month to arrive, by which time the Boston winter should have set in, ensuring that he had a supply of ice.

Once he had bade William and James farewell, Frederic set to work to prepare for the collection and shipping of the ice. It was a lonely and difficult time for him. Many people had by now discovered what he was up to, and were making fun of him. He wrote defiantly in his diary, "Let those who win laugh." His father urged him to cut his losses and stay in Boston: "Every person is in wondering mood at our going to the West Indies and the Judge is continually told what a pity it is and how dangerous too and what a miserable prospect there is of success and I have a lecture every morning urging me to abandon the voyage which he says without knowing our plan is wild and ruinous."

Had Frederic known what William and James were experiencing, he might have taken more notice of this advice; it was not all plain sailing onboard the *Jane*, and there were hazards enough at the end of the voyage. James kept some notes of their adventures, which he later wrote up in the form of a diary. It is perhaps significant that there is not a single mention in his account of what anybody thought about their ice enterprise— did he himself take it seriously? Frederic certainly doubted the commitment of both his cousin and his brother.

By Wednesday, November 27, the *Jane* had gone through some rough weather, but was expected to reach St. Pierre by Sunday of the following week. On Saturday, James noted: "We have spread all sail with a fine fresh breeze and strained our eyes 'to see what was not to be seen.' " As they scanned the horizon for a glimpse of land, they saw instead another ship bearing down on them from the northeast. "We feared she was a Spanish privateer and dreaded being plundered and ill-treated; or she might be English and order us to another island, altho' our papers are fair." Though the great age of piracy in these seas had ended a century earlier, there were still privateers waylaying ships with a view to stealing what they could. At first James's fears appeared to be justified, for the ship fired across their bows as a signal to hove to. They were asked where they had sailed from and where they were going. The captain of the *Jane* was ordered aboard the ship, which, according to James, was "a handsome schooner with men of all colors on board." To everyone's great relief, the captain returned within a quarter of an hour to report that it was a French privateer just out from Martinique, and that he had been well treated—in fact, he had been offered fruit and liqueurs.

They were sent on their way, and shortly afterward had sight of land. The next day, as they headed for the port of St. Pierre, they were stopped again. This time it was an English ship, the *Nimrod*, which put another shot across their bows. Again they were treated with civility and allowed to sail on. When they were close enough to the island to make out cultivated fields along the shore, a third vessel, this time a "small topsail schooner," came alongside and sent a boat to ask who they were and where they were going. The schooner then slid away, toward the coast. Evening was drawing in and they could see firing in the distance, but had no idea who was involved in the skirmish.

As they were cruising into the harbor, a shore battery fired two shots that landed close to them. Then, James wrote, "We hung a lantern in the main shrouds and were safe." The *Jane* weighed anchor the following morning, December 4. William and James found lodgings and took a look around St. Pierre, which impressed them. "Through every street runs a stream of water, which conveys all the filth from the houses to the sea, and at the same time produced a constant agitation of the air," James noted with admiration. The town already had a form of air-conditioning, it seems. But would it ever get a supply of ice cream?

Before William and James had arrived in St. Pierre, Frederic had already sent them a letter with the news that he had his eye on an ideal vessel for transporting the ice, a brig named the *Favorite*. He had looked it over just after they had set sail. On November 27, he noted in his diary that he had bought it for $4,750, a considerable sum of money and the best part of his entire capital, which he had raised by mortgaging some of the land he had bought in the South Boston scheme. For a merchant to purchase a ship to carry a single cargo was very unusual; the normal practice was to buy space on a ship and pay a freight charge to its owner. The newspapers had columns of advertisements inviting merchants to buy space on ships destined for particular ports.

Although there is no mention of it in his diary, the reason Frederic went to the expense of becoming a shipowner was because nobody wanted to carry his ice. What kind of cargo was it that would start to melt as soon as it was loaded? Most ships, whether they were going to China or India or plying the coastal trade, carried a mix of cargoes, and a hold full of melt-water and slush could ruin all the cargo. The ice was heavy, and would therefore weigh down the ship and act initially as ballast; but as it drained away into the sea, the ship would become lighter and less easy to handle. Whether or not Frederic was able to get any quotes for freighting ice we do not know, but it is unlikely. There was, anyway, another reason for buying a brig: as the owner, Frederic could fit it out as he wished, and he knew that to carry ice its hold would have to be lined with boards to provide a crude form of insulation. Buying a ship in Boston at that time was as easy as slapping down a few thousand dollars for a secondhand truck would be today, but the *Favorite* was Frederic's single largest investment in this first venture, and the cost of it would absorb any profit he managed to make.

There was nothing much Frederic could do other than wait for news from William and James and for the winter to set in. A contact in Philadelphia sent him a copy of a pamphlet titled "An essay on the Most Eligible Construction of Ice Houses and a Description of the Newly Invented Refrigerator," written by a Maryland farmer and engineer named Thomas Moore. It had been published two years earlier, in 1803, and was an indication that Americans other than Frederic Tudor were thinking about how to make better and more profitable use of natural ice. Moore's essay was written for farmers who still brought their butter to market at night during the summer months, and often had to sell it at a reduced price the following morning after it had melted. Moore urged them to build more efficient ice-houses, and to make themselves refrigerators that would keep their butter hard on even the hottest day. His own patented design was a wooden box with a tin lining and layers of insulation, including rabbit fur, which would preserve ice for a whole day. There had been earlier models of refrigerators, but Moore thought his the most efficient. Frederic does not appear to have been as impressed by Moore's essay as he might have been. He was evolving his own ideas about how best to build icehouses, but had not thought much about how his customers on Martinique might preserve the ice they bought from him—an oversight that was to cause him considerable anxiety.

After two days in lodgings in St. Pierre, William and James were taken in by the Moneau family, fugitives from the French Revolution who had fled to South Carolina, then moved to Martinique. The two cultured young men from Boston who spoke tolerable French were a social success, and within a week were granted two interviews with the Prefect, who they believed could arrange for exclusive rights to sell ice on the island. They sent a letter to Frederic telling of their safe arrival and warm welcome. However, both suffered bouts of fever, and only James was well enough to present their case when they were called for an interview. By Christmas Eve, it appeared that they had succeeded: their petition had been granted in the name of the Emperor Napoleon, and they could collect the signed papers the next day. But what appeared to be a fine Christmas present turned out to have a price on it: about four hundred dollars. They were also asked to give an account of how ice sales in Martinique would proceed, a subject on which they were even vaguer than Frederic. With the whole venture in jeopardy, they decided to soften up the prefect with a bribe. As they could not find the official himself, they left a letter and two gold coins known as "Joes," a Portuguese currency, and worth considerably less than four hundred dollars, at the home of his secretary. The following day they had their monopoly with no conditions and no fees asked. They wrote immediately to Frederic with the good news in a letter dated December 26.

Frederic received William and James's first letter, telling of their arrival, on January 10, 1806. Quite unaware of the difficulties they had encountered, he noted in his diary the "highly pleasing" news that they had been "received into the first company of the Island and met with the most flattering salutations." On the same day, he wrote: "It has now begun to freeze for the first time this winter. The Brig is all ready and the sky looks bright for the success of the scheme!"

By that time, James was bedridden, struck down by yellow fever in the home of an old friend who lived in the town of Les Trois Islets. After two weeks, William left him alone to continue the West Indies tour. He took a ship to the island of Guadeloupe, then on to Antigua, all the while sounding out the market for Boston ice. He had no idea how Frederic was getting on, and it appears to have been no part of the plan to greet him on his arrival on Martinique.

On January 20, Frederic received William and James's second letter, with the good news that exclusive rights had been granted and that there was an agent awaiting the arrival of the ice. But the sky was no longer bright for the success of the scheme. Frederic wrote in his diary:

> Everything except the weather favors the enterprise.
> This is indeed most remarkably bad—nothing but storm,

frost and snow, it is certainly a difficult thing to see the moment for getting the ice and putting it on board there has not been one opportunity yet. Either the harbor has been frozen up or when open there was no ice. Storms have twice already prevented cutting the ice and when the storm ceases the pond is covered with snow.

The possibility that the weather might not be favorable had not been anticipated, even though Boston's winter climate was notoriously variable, with huge leaps and falls in temperature. Frederic had nowhere to store ice when it was eventually cut, and was hoping that it could go straight to the ship and on to Martinique without delay. But ships were sometimes icebound in Boston Harbor in winter, and it had not occurred to Frederic that weather that produced good ice on Rockwood Pond might also prevent the *Favorite* from sailing. All in all, the technicalities of cutting and shipping ice were proving to be much more problematic than he had foreseen. It would be interesting to know where and how Frederic planned to harvest upward of a hundred tons of ice, but he does not say. As he refers to "the pond," perhaps he meant Rockwood Pond on the family estate. But he might also have contracted with local farmers to get additional supplies, as he certainly did later on. We do not know who cut his ice, but presumably it was hacked and sawn out, delivered to his ship in irregular blocks by horse-drawn wagon, then thrown or lowered into the specially prepared hold and sealed over with some hay as insulation.

It was already the end of the first week in February 1806 when Frederic felt confident enough to provision his ship, paying $5.75 for rum, brandy, and other essentials. Captain Thomas

Pearson was engaged for fifty dollars a month. The ice was cut and the ship loaded and ready to sail by February 10. They were bade farewell by the *Boston Gazette*, which expressed the whole mercantile community's derision in three sentences:

> No joke. A vessel with a cargo of 80 tons of Ice has cleared out from this port for Martinique. We hope this will not prove to be a slippery speculation.

Bad weather kept the *Favorite* in harbor until February 13, but then she made good passage and arrived in St. Pierre on March 5, a voyage of only twenty-one days. According to Frederic, when she left Boston she had onboard not 80 but 130 tons of ice, though exact measurements were hardly relevant—what was important was how much was left when he got to Martinique. This he did not record, stating only that the ice that did survive the trip was in "perfect condition"—an odd description, as ice in any other state would presumably have disappeared. He certainly had a considerable quantity left, but found he had nowhere in St. Pierre to store it. He put the blame for this on William and James, who had left a letter for him suggesting sites for an icehouse, although none was ready. They also gave the names of nine prominent people who expected complimentary blocks of ice—"as much as a negro could carry"—and the captain-general should be sent a hundred pounds of it. An agent named William Dawson had a copy of the privilege that had been granted, but William and James advised Frederic not to bother staying on Martinique, as there did not seem to be much demand for ice there.

All he could do was seek permission to sell his ice directly from the *Favorite*, though this meant that it would melt rapidly when the hold was open. He sold fifty dollars' worth in two days, charging sixteen cents a pound. He was offered four thousand dollars for the whole cargo, but decided to turn this down. To draw in more customers, he had printed some handbills that were distributed in St. Pierre. He kept a copy and later pasted it in his icehouse diary. Headed "Glace," it announced in French that from that day, March 7, and for the following three days, small quantities of ice would be sold aboard ship from a well-preserved consignment brought from Boston on the brig *Favorite,* and that after three days, the brig would move on to another island. The price was thirty French sous per pound. Buyers were advised to bring a woolen cloth or some other material to wrap around the ice they bought in order to preserve it.

There were no refrigerators in St. Pierre, and according to Frederic, most islanders had no idea what to do with the ice once they had bought it. This inhibited sales, and business was sluggish. Frederic was in a state of great anxiety, and ready to blame everyone but himself for the predicament he was in. He wrote to his brother-in-law Robert Gardiner:

It is difficult to conceive how determined to believe most of the people here are that ice will melt in spite of all pre-cautions; and their methods of keeping it are laughable, to be sure. One carries it through the street to his house in the sun noonday, puts it in a plate before his door, and then complains that "il fond." Another puts it in a tub of water, a third by way of climax puts his in salt! And all this not-withstanding they were directed in the handbill what to do.

Frederic does not say what he expected the islanders to do with a few small lumps of ice that would melt rapidly whether or not they were wrapped in a blanket en route from the *Favorite* to their homes. His best trade, it seems, was making ice cream, and in his letter to Robert Gardiner he told of one small triumph:

> The man who keeps the Tivoli Garden insisted ice creams could not be made in this country and that the ice itself would all thaw before he could get it home! I told him I had made them here . . . and putting my fist pretty hard upon the table I called . . . for an order of 60lbs of ice and in a pretty warm tone directed the man to have his cream ready and that I would come to freeze it for him in the morning, which I did accordingly, being determined to spare no pains to convince these people that they cannot only have ice but all the luxuries arising here as elsewhere. The Tivoli man rec'd for these creams the first night $300; after this he was humble as a mushroom.

Frederic's account of his first attempt to sell ice in the West Indies is not entirely convincing. It is very unlikely that when the *Favorite* docked in St. Pierre his ice was, as he claimed, "in perfect condition." A considerable portion of the cargo would have melted on the voyage, as at that time, he did not know how to insulate it really effectively. He must have realized as soon as the *Favorite* weighed anchor that he was not going to sell ten thousand dollars' worth of ice, as he had hoped, and from the very beginning he was cutting his losses. He should have accepted the offer of four thousand dollars for the entire shipment and found a cargo for the return voyage, for which he could at least charge freight. Instead he hung on, selling about twenty to thirty dollars' worth of ice a day. He had no idea where William and James were, and had nowhere to sail on to.

Toward the end of March, with the ice melting faster than he could sell it, Frederic accepted a proposition that he take a cargo of sugar back to Boston, and that the remaining ice be unloaded and sold on commission. In the meantime, he sailed the 120 miles southeast to Barbados, hoping to get the same kind of exclusive privilege he had on Martinique. He was unsuccessful, and by the time he returned to St. Pierre, all his ice had gone and the *Favorite* was loaded with sugar and ready to sail. Two hours out of port the brig hit a squall and lost her masts, which had only recently been repaired. The disconsolate Frederic had to return to St. Pierre, where he was given a compensatory box of oranges by the man who had sold the last of his ice on commission. It was not until late April that he finally headed back to Boston, with a paragraph from a St. Pierre newspaper as a keepsake:

> It will be a remarkable epoch in the history of luxury and enterprise that on the 6th March ice creams have been eaten in Martinique probably for the first time since the settlement of the country. And this too in a volcanic land lying 14 degrees north of the equator.

When he got home, Frederic pasted this proudly into his ice-house diary.

William and James were still on their tour of the West Indies when the *Favorite* left St. Pierre. James's yellow fever had laid him low for seven weeks, and he did not meet up with William again until the end of February, on the island of St. Croix, near Puerto Rico. From there they sailed to Jamaica, where the English governor, Sir Eyre Coote, heard their case for exclusive rights to supply the island with ice. Sir Eyre was courteous, according to William, "though he thought it a cursed strange thing." Throughout the British Empire, however, only the privy council in London could grant exclusive trade deals.

The ice envoys did not set sail for Boston until May 4, when they boarded the *Huntress*, which was loaded with seventy hogsheads of high-proof rum. They were once again waylaid by privateers, including a Spanish ship, which gave them the most unpleasant reception of the whole voyage. An officer came aboard rattling a cutlass and ordered everyone to disembark and to go onboard the privateer. When some of them, including James, were slow to obey, the officer waved the cutlass above their heads, and gave James a tap on the shoulder with the blunt edge. They later discovered that while on the privateer they had been robbed of a few valuables, including William's set of pistols and two gold watches. After that, the *Huntress* made slow progress, as the captain had trouble establishing his position. On May 15, when they discovered they were farther away from Boston than they had been the day before, James scribbled a note: "Ah! what a glorious fellow will he be who can discover a mode of finding Longitude, easy, certain and expeditious, as that of ascertaining Latitude." A clock that kept good time at sea and was unaffected by changes in weather and atmosphere was what was needed. Chronometers had been made by the Englishman John Harrison more than thirty years earlier, but do not appear to have been in use in New England in the early 1800s.

After a few days in quarantine in Boston Harbor—to guard against the importation of yellow fever and smallpox—William and James set foot again on New England soil on June 3. They had been away for six months. Frederic was not at all pleased with their efforts, and showed no sympathy for the illness James had suffered. Instead he wrote in his diary:

> The advantages derived from their part of the expedition were not equal to the expense of it, which was near $2,000. They never entered into the undertaking with the ardor which was necessary to insure success in the outset of the business. They were easily discouraged and did not announce the thing with that confidence that defies ridicule and opposition, insures friends and leads in every project more than anything to success. I make no apology to myself for expressing here my private opinions as it is for myself alone I minute down here all the circumstances attending the undertaking which I projected. If I am so unfortunate as to have connected with me friends who have not aided me, let them if they ever read what I am now writing remember that I only blame them for not understanding "how to conduct a new and as the world says extravagant enterprise."

Frederic calculated that the losses from this first venture in the ice trade amounted to between three and four thousand dollars, with total ice sales of about two thousand. However, he reasoned that he was not responsible for this setback, and that though the first shipment of ice had proved to be a costly failure, he now knew how to make it pay. In fact, he was already planning his next venture, this time to Havana.

3

From the Icehouse to the Jailhouse

Frederic Tudor had had a miserable time in Martinique: he had lost a great deal of money, and he regarded his brother and cousin as half-hearted business associates. Yet he did not abandon his dream of making a fortune selling ice. Why he was so persistent is a mystery, for the prospect before him was not at all promising, and there were many other commodities he might have traded in. The icehouse diaries he kept almost continuously from 1805 until 1838 do not really provide a satisfactory answer. What they do reveal is a blind commitment to a venture that many times threatened Frederic's health and sanity, and often caused him acute embarrassment within the Boston community. He had bouts of self-pity, but rarely of self-doubt. What drove him on even when everything seemed hopeless was his pride: he had announced to the world at the age of twenty-two that he could make money out of a commodity other New Englanders regarded as worthless, and he was determined to prove that he was right and all those around him were wrong.

Frederic's dismay at the apparent bafflement of the people of St. Pierre when offered a chunk of ice did not undermine his belief that there was a ready market for it in hot climates. Once they became accustomed to regular deliveries, he felt, people would be hooked. The same would be true in Havana and possibly southern U.S. cities such as Charleston and New Orleans. Nobody could doubt that this luxury would be sought after if there were guaranteed deliveries to cover the hottest months of the year. And a lesson Frederic had learned from the unsuccessful expedition to Martinique was that there must be a properly designed icehouse at the point of delivery, from which small quantities could be sold over weeks or even months.

In August 1806, Frederic's brother William sailed from New York to London to pursue the grant of exclusive ice-trade rights with British-owned islands in the West Indies. The Judge, along with Frederic's mother and younger sister Delia, followed him. They intended to enjoy the glamorous social round in England and France and, with luck, find a good match for Delia. However, it was already becoming clear that the family was in serious financial difficulty. The Judge's South Boston speculation was not yet returning any kind of profit, and he had to sell some of his property and borrow money at a high interest rate to fund the trip to Europe.

Frederic had no money either, and was unable to find any financial backers for the ice venture. His brig the *Favorite* is not mentioned again in his diaries, and he must have sold it—almost certainly at a loss, for it had needed extensive repairs in Martinique. In future, he would have to persuade shipowners to carry his unconventional cargo. This would prove to be less of a problem, as the voyage to Martinique had demonstrated that it was feasible, and would not sink a vessel.

Throughout the summer and autumn, Frederic spent his time making contacts in the West Indies, setting up agents on Jamaica, Barbados, Guadeloupe, and St. Thomas. He arranged for an icehouse to be built in St. Pierre. He had a good contact in Havana, for his cousin William Savage, James's brother, lived there. Though William failed to persuade the Spanish authorities to grant exclusive rights to sell ice in Cuba, he was able to get an icehouse of sorts built in Havana.

When the first hard frosts of the winter froze Rockwood Pond in January 1807, Frederic began his second season in the ice trade. The technology of harvesting and shipping ice was still very crude; he probably supplemented what he could get from Rockwood with supplies bought from local farmers. Though he had been working on designs for an icehouse at Rockwood, Frederic still had nowhere to hold large reserves that might last through the summer. His shipping would be done in winter and spring, when the temperature in Boston, though very variable, would preserve the ice until it was sent south. Though he would have to pay for the building of icehouses and freight charges if the trade expanded, the ice itself was free: nobody owned the frozen water of the New England ponds, and he could get supplies wherever he wanted. One excellent source of good, clear ice was Fresh Pond in Cambridge, and Frederic almost certainly paid a winter workforce to cut ice from there.

In January 1807, Frederic sent his second cargo of ice to the West Indies, but he did not sail with it. This time it went to Havana, to be stored and sold by his cousin William Savage. There were about 180 tons of ice onboard the brig *Trident* when it left Boston. We do not know how much of this survived the voyage, but William was able to fill the Havana icehouse, and he found a ready market, chiefly among the café owners, who used it to make chilled drinks and ice cream. In March and April, two more consignments of ice were sent, and though the ice lasted only about two weeks in Havana, William was able to sell six thousand dollars' worth. With William, Frederic arranged for the *Trident* to ship a cargo of molasses from Havana on the voyage back to Boston. This would have been profitable had the customer paid up, but his business failed and Frederic had to foot the bill. He could not afford to send another shipment of ice to Martinique, and his new icehouse there was abandoned.

Meanwhile, William Tudor was involved in difficult negotiations with the British authorities in London. He had good contacts there, but nobody could quite believe that he really was asking for exclusive rights to sell ice to West Indian islands. They suspected that this was a cover, and a particularly bizarre one at that, for some Yankee smuggling operation. William had to come up with some special reason to persuade the authorities that the ice trade would be useful to the British in the West Indies. He found it in the claim that ice would be of great medical benefit in the treatment of fevers. A doctor's letter arguing the case for ice-pack treatment secured the deal, and William was able to inform Frederic that he had the monopoly he wanted in Jamaica, Antigua, and Barbados. But by this time, he could not afford to pay for any ice shipments, and the hard-won exclusive privileges were worthless.

In the second year of the ice trade, Frederic had made only three shipments to Havana, and the prospects there, though promising, were limited by the rapid melting of his cargo once it was landed. He decided to go to Havana himself and build a better icehouse in preparation for his third season. Though he did not know it when he first arrived in Cuba in mid-December 1807, his journey was a waste of time and money. The American president, Thomas Jefferson, had persuaded Congress to put a temporary stop on all shipments from American ports as a demonstration of the new nation's neutrality in European conflict. Frederic was left high and dry; he abandoned his half-built icehouse in Havana and sailed back to Boston, as he would be unable to make any shipments that winter.

He had not been back at Rockwood long when his father returned from Europe alone, leaving his wife, son, and daughter behind. The family fortune was gone, and what hope there was of retrieving it was locked up in the South Boston venture, the outcome of which remained uncertain. The Judge needed to find work, and through friends obtained an official position in the office of the secretary of state for Massachusetts, which gave him some income and a modest social status. He and Frederic still believed that the South Boston venture could return a hundred thousand dollars. In fact, all the Judge got back was nine thousand. Frederic was deeply affected by the decline in his family's fortunes, and was determined to save them from impending poverty.

Though he could not ship any ice that winter, Frederic did not abandon the venture, as he might well have done. He was still convinced that if he could overcome the problem of how to preserve ice efficiently in hot climates, there were good profits to be made. In the summer of 1808, he had time on his hands and a supply of ice in the Rockwood icehouse with which he could experiment. Why ice kept better in some conditions than others was a mystery. Obviously, some materials would provide better insulation than others, and Frederic needed something that would be available in bulk and was not too expensive. He had at hand plenty of charcoal and some light, spongy peat, which was also used as fuel at Rockwood. To determine which might be the better insulator, he took two large wooden casks, put pulverized charcoal in one and peat in the other, filled them with ice, and put the lids on. Forty days later, when he opened the casks, the ice had melted in both of them—this was between mid-June and the end of July—but the meltwater was warm in the barrel insulated with charcoal and cool in the peat barrel. He carried out the experiment again, opening the casks sooner, and found that some ice remained in the peat barrel whereas it had all melted in the charcoal barrel. Peat, although the poorer fuel, was the better insulator.

In Frederic's mind at this time was the notion that if he could create a thriving industry from otherwise valueless ice and cheap insulating material, he would have cracked a problem that all New Englanders faced. Because they lacked resources of their own to export, and their rivers, running north to south, did not connect them to the developing interior of the country, they were dependent on the sea and trade along the East Coast or far overseas for their prosperity. But quite often, when a cargo had been discharged on the wharves at Boston, there was nothing in bulk to carry on an outward voyage. Ships were designed to sail with a full hold, and were unstable and difficult to handle without a cargo. If there was no salable ballast, something had to be found to weight the ship down, and would be jettisoned at the end of the outward voyage. In Boston, stones were dredged from the bay, which was time-consuming and therefore costly. But if a vessel took on ice rather than stones, there would be a freight charge paid to the shipper. A shipowner who might otherwise have loaded with worthless ballast had an incentive to take ice even at a very low rate, provided he was convinced that this unusual cargo would not damage his vessel.

Although Frederic was the butt of much wry humor when he first tried to sell ice, the venture was considered in later years as typically "Yankee," because it was making something out of nothing. And in retrospect, the ice trade made more sense in the peculiar economy of Massachusetts than even Frederic at first realized. He was later to claim credit for reviving the flagging Boston trade with India, because his ice at least gave the shippers a freight income on their long outward journey. It was just as true, of course, that if ballast had not been a problem for Boston shipowners, the ice trade would probably never have become established, for frozen water was not the most lucrative cargo to carry.

Although he had made little money from them, Frederic had proved the feasibility of the ice trade with his first four shipments. The ice lasted, the ships were undamaged, and there was a market for cool drinks and ice cream in tropical climates. Taking into account the cost of harvesting the ice, carrying it to a wharf on Boston's Charlestown quays, a modest freight charge, and all other expenses, including the building of icehouses, it seemed that a profit could be made. However, if enjoying ice was to become an established luxury in the West Indies, supplies would have to be regular. When he sought exclusive rights to sell ice, Frederic would argue that if he was guaranteed sales and was free of troublesome competition, he would be better able to establish regular shipments. That was what he hoped for in Cuba, but in 1808 there was no point in pursuing an exclusive deal because no ships were sailing.* To add to his frustration, his brother William returned from Europe with the news that in France he had been granted a Napoleonic privilege to trade with France's West Indian islands.

The shipping embargo was to last until the spring of 1809, and Frederic did not bother to harvest any ice for export the previous winter. However, he and William imagined for a short time that they had chanced upon another speculation that would save them and the family from penury. William had taken his watch to be repaired, and learned from the watchmaker that coal had been found in remote land on Cape Cod and the island of Martha's Vineyard. If there were coal deposits in New

---

*This was a result of the Embargo Act of 1807, an attempt by the United States to impose economic sanctions on the British, who were preventing neutral American ships from trading with France and were impressing U.S. seamen. President Jefferson forbade any trade by American ships away from East Coast ports. This did some damage to British interests, but far more to American shipping. The embargo was lifted in 1809.

England, they could be worth their weight in gold, and Frederic became very excited. As with the ice venture, he wanted as few people as possible to know about this find. He asked his father for some funds to explore Martha's Vineyard and look into the purchase of mineral rights, but the Judge had no money unless he mortgaged Rockwood, and the venture was too risky for that. But Frederic managed to put together a kind of mining company with a committee of six that included his cousin William Savage, back from Havana.

Three of this committee, including Frederic and his cousin William, disguised as hunters, set out to explore the prospective coal mines. They took their guns and let it be known they were going to do some shooting. Frederic had been fond of the outdoor life since boyhood, and this was a not implausible cover story. They sailed to Cape Cod, where they found coal specimens, and hired a schooner to take them to Martha's Vineyard. Here they collected more specimens, in weather that rapidly deteriorated and drove them to put up for the night at an inn. The next day they hired a boatman to take them back to Boston through treacherous seas that were running high. They were very nearly shipwrecked, and had to drop their sails and row eleven miles, through the night, to make shore. But the venture came to nothing. They had found coal, and a lease to dig for it was obtained from the Native Americans who owned the land, but they had no money to take it any further.

The Tudors were at a very low ebb, driven back to their Rockwood estate. It had been left to them as a place to spend happy summer months; now it was their last resort. As a farm, it was in a sorry state, with two horses, two yoke of oxen, two cows, one heifer, three hogs, and fifty chickens. Because the family had no inclination to run the farm themselves, they had hired two people to do the work, and their annual wages of five hundred dollars was more than the total income from the sale of hay, corn, potatoes, and carrots. Rockwood ice was potentially the most valuable crop on the farm—with the possible exception of Frederic's sister Delia, who was now of marriageable age. Delia had been courted by some respectably wealthy young men, but to Frederic's annoyance had turned them down, and now she was spending what little Tudor money was left on a European jaunt with her mother.

In the autumn of 1809, Frederic's only hope of financial salvation was the forthcoming ice harvest. He was aware that few if any Boston merchants regarded his enterprise as worth pursuing, and he must have felt very self-conscious as he mingled with them on their customary trading ground on State Street, where he would go still hoping to find backers. Then, late in 1809, he was approached on State Street by a sheriff and, in full view of Boston's mercantile community, was put under arrest for debt. A creditor had waited long enough for payment. The debt laws were harsh, and Frederic expected to be marched straight to jail. However, as it was his first offense, he was given a reprieve: if he repaid the money within a week, he would not be put behind bars. Somehow the Judge and a few friends raised enough to save Frederic from prison. But he was mortified, and wrote to his brother-in-law Robert Gardiner that the experience had been "abominable."

As the weather was hardening, it was time for Frederic to plan his next season of ice sales to Havana. He decided to go himself, leaving William Savage in Boston to organize the harvesting and loading. This would enable Frederic to escape the social embarrassment he suffered in Boston and to continue his plan to build a more efficient icehouse, though just what his design improvements were at this stage is not clear. After a good deal of negotiation and the payment of a few bribes when he got to Havana, he secured his monopoly. The following April, two cargoes of ice arrived from Boston, and they sold well, bringing in $5,600 by August. In May, a shipment of ice by a rival arrived in Havana—there is no record of who sent it—but Frederic was able to crow in his diary that "he made so poor a hand of it that after some days he threw his ice overboard and I encountered no further difficulties in my sales." It would be interesting to know more about this incident, but we only have Frederic's curt account. From later reports of his tactics for seeing off rivals, it is probable that he simply put a very low price on his ice for long enough to undermine his competitor's sales. As nobody else had icehouses as efficient as his, they could not keep their cargo for long, and their profits would simply melt away. If they sold at the same price as Frederic, they would not make a profit and would be discouraged from continuing in the trade.

The Havana venture was looking promising; then Frederic caught yellow fever. He sailed back to Boston in August, leaving another cousin, Arthur Savage, in charge of ice sales, which at the end of the season totaled $7,400. The 1810 season had proved to be the first that returned a profit. When expenses were paid, it was a mere thousand dollars, but, as Frederic noted in his diary, that year "must forever remain a monument of the advantage of steady perseverance in a project that is good in the main." His optimism appeared to be justified as the next season got under way. He put an agent in charge in Havana, and stayed in Boston to handle shipments.

In 1811, Frederic sent his younger brother, Harry, then twenty years old, to Kingston, Jamaica, with the aim of setting up an ice trade there. Harry was regarded by most of the family as an idler and a good-for-nothing, and this would be a way of getting him to do something useful. True to form, he overslept on the day he was supposed to sail to Jamaica and missed the boat. When he finally got there, he demanded more money than Frederic wanted to pay. The first shipment of ice to Jamaica left Boston in April 1811 on the schooner *Active,* but it never reached Harry. When Frederic heard the news that the *Active* had been shipwrecked and all the ice lost, he was more relieved than disappointed, for it meant he did not have to pay the freight charge, which would probably have been greater than the profit from the ice. That, for the time being, was the end of the Jamaica venture and of Harry's introduction to the ice trade.

In early March 1812, Frederic still owed money to a number of people in Boston, and was having difficulty settling all his debts on time. It would take only one of his creditors to go to the law and Frederic would be marched off to prison. That was what now happened. In his diary, on March 14, he wrote:

On Monday the 9th instant I was arrested . . . and locked up as a debtor in Boston jail . . . On this memorable day in my little annals I am 28 years 6 months and 5 days old. It is an event which I think I could not have avoided:

but it is a climax which I did hope to have escaped as my affairs are looking well at last after a fearful struggle with adverse circumstances for seven years—but it has taken place and I have endeavored to meet it as I would the tempest of heaven which should serve to strengthen rather than reduce the spirit of a true man.

Buoyed by his own fine sentiments, Frederic gathered together the money to pay off the debt and was out of jail in time to arrange another ice shipment to Havana. He also established a basement store for ice in Boston, as it was becoming obvious that he needed to retain supplies there during the summer if he was going to ship cargoes on a regular basis. By juggling his precarious financial affairs, he managed to keep going, though he was aware that he owed a great deal more than he owned.

He might just have survived had fate not once again dealt him an unfair hand. Just when he had his Boston cellars stocked with ice, there was another embargo on American trade, this time as a result of the conflict with Britain that became known as the War of 1812, the origins of which are still a matter of dispute, but which stemmed from continuing tensions between the United States and Britain after the American Revolution. What was not in doubt was that Frederic had to abandon the Havana trade and allow his ice to melt away unsold. By July, he was in deep financial trouble. The family still had some assets: Rockwood, the land in South Boston, and the house in town were worth around $28,400. But Frederic owed a number of people, including his blacksmith and his tailor, a total of $38,772.

There was to be no ice trade the coming winter, and Frederic had no money to develop the coal-mining venture. But he reasoned that as America was at war, a new and faster ship might be an asset, and he had just the design. He had always fancied himself an inventor, though he had no professional skills to call upon. The key to his revolutionary concept was a ship that had a keel only at the stern, rather than running the length of the boat. He wrote to President Jefferson and to the secretary of the navy with an account of his design, but received no reply. Surprisingly, given Frederic's reputation in Boston at that time, he found a shipyard prepared to build a prototype and backers to pay for it. He christened the ship, which was 66 feet long and weighed 130 tons, the *Black Swan*. If it proved successful, Frederic would be able to profit from the sale of his design.

The *Black Swan*, built by Barker's shipyard in Charlestown, was ready for launching the following spring. On May 1, 1813, it made its maiden voyage up the Charles River, with Frederic proudly on deck. It had not gone far when a Boston sheriff came aboard with a demand that Frederic repay a debt of three hundred dollars. He could not come up with the money, and was once again put behind bars. Of this experience he wrote much later:

> The jail was an old one and the room in which they put me had no chair in it. It did not smell very sweet: but there was a long bench which I pulled into the middle and laid down upon my back to reflect upon what was to be done next. I smiled to think that any one should believe I was beaten, or in the slightest degree daunted in the steady purpose I had formed of accomplishing the payment of every dollar of debt and lifting myself to lord it over, if I chose, my humble creditor and his instrument. I never doubted I should accomplish what I have accomplished.

The *Black Swan* did not impress in its trials, and was never tested on the high seas; but as it turned out, the winds of war did blow Frederic one mixed blessing in the form of a fiery sea captain named Charles Stewart, who emerged from the conflict as a husband for sister Delia. Frederic had ordered her and his mother to return to Boston just as the war was breaking out, not for their safety so much as to put an end to their extravagances, for which he was footing the bill. They had been back just under a year when in June 1813 Captain Stewart arrived in Boston to take command of the United States frigate *Constitution*, which had to undergo repairs. A small, convivial, red-haired Irishman, he met Delia and showed some interest in her. Frederic, believing Stewart to be just what the family needed, goaded his sister into ensnaring him. They were married on November 25, 1813, a month before Stewart set off to sea. It was by all accounts a disastrous union of a rough seaman and a cultured Boston lady, and no recommendation for Frederic's gifts as a matchmaker. But it meant Delia was no longer a drain on his uncertain resources.

In the summer of 1814, in a desperate attempt to raise more capital, Frederic considered mortgaging Rockwood and apportioning the proceeds among the family. But his mother demanded a much larger share than he would allow, and the project was dropped. Arrested three times for debt, jailed twice, his ice trade suspended by war, Frederic was in a desperate situation.

Meanwhile, Captain Stewart proved a very able commander, and when the war ended in December 1814, he returned to Boston a hero of many successes against the British (he did not, in fact, learn until April 1815 that the war was over, and went on attacking British warships during several months of peace). He was feted in New York, presented with a commemorative sword in Philadelphia, and took the lion's share of the forty thousand dollars awarded by Congress to the officers and crew of the *Constitution* for the capture of a British naval ship. Naturally enough, Frederic fancied that some of this money might be invested in his next venture in the frozen-water trade. Stewart had encouraged the idea that he might help Frederic, suggesting to him a number of ventures he considered worth an investment. But it turned out that ice was not one of them, and Frederic got nowhere with his brother-in-law, despite a persistent campaign of letter writing.

On January 18, 1814, Frederic had confided to his diary:

> I complain of hard destiny, and have I not reason? If it were constitutional habit, I should despise myself. I have manfully maintained as long as I possibly could that "success is virtue." I say so still; but my heart tells me I don't believe it. Have I not been industrious? Have not many of my calculations been good? And have not all my undertakings in the eventful Ice business been attended by a villainous train of events against which no calculation could be made which have heretofore prevented success which must have followed if only the common chances and changes of this world had not happened against me? They have worried me. They have cured me of superfluous gaiety. They have made my head gray; but they have not driven me to despair.

It was in this defiant mood that Frederic prepared the following autumn to resume the ice trade. He was becoming adept at avoiding the attentions of Boston sheriffs armed with warrants for the execution of debt, and managed to load up a ship and slip out of port on November 1, 1815, bound for Havana. His mother, perhaps a little repentant about demanding too large a share of the proposed Rockwood mortgage, sent him some candy and a few shirts to see him on his way. Frederic, destitute and still living the life of a single man in a boardinghouse, did not thank her. He had only one thing on his mind: the new and revolutionary icehouse he was going to construct in Havana that would finally set the trade on a proper footing and make him his fortune.

4

Exile in Havana

Frederic did not like Havana: the climate was oppressive, he thought the "grossness of the people extreme," he had constant trouble with the authorities, and yellow fever was rampant.* But it had been the best market for his ice, and he had no alternative but to try to reestablish his trade there. With each new venture he had made improvements in the technology of the frozen-water trade, and as he sailed to Cuba in November 1815, he had onboard the materials to build a brand-new and revolutionary icehouse. He also took with him the Boston carpenters who would put it together.

*At the time, Cuba was controlled by the Spanish, who had exchanged Florida for it in a deal with the British in 1763. The island had a thriving trade, exporting coffee, tobacco, and sugar to the United States. In 1817, Cuba's population was five hundred thousand, more than half of whom were black, many of them still enslaved. Havana was a bustling port with pleasure gardens and coffeehouses, but the Spanish colonial society was regarded as rough and ready compared with that of New England.

Though the merchants and investors in Boston were yet to be convinced that the ice trade would pay, Frederic did now have agents who would provide him with regular supplies of ice, so he could leave that side of the business to them. Before he escaped Boston, pursued by a sheriff with yet another warrant for his arrest for debt, he had arranged for a shipment of ice that would arrive in Havana sometime in March. That would give him plenty of time to get his icehouse prepared. Or so he imagined.

Frederic arrived in Havana on November 27, and from the moment he made contact with the partner he had found there, a man named Nathaniel Fellows, it was apparent that reestablishing the ice trade was not going to be an easy matter. It is a wonder that he survived the misfortunes that beset him. Had he not done so, it is doubtful that the ice trade would have become established in North America, for the few competitors he had at this time regarded ice as not much more than a superior form of ballast, and had no notion of creating a regular business in harvesting and shipping it. Only Frederic Tudor had the vision and the crazy determination to make it work.

The first thing he discovered on his arrival in Havana was that he had a rival who claimed it was he, not Tudor, who had a monopoly on ice sales to Cuba. This interloper, a Spanish adventurer named Carlos Goberto de Ceta, also tried to persuade the authorities that he could free the island from its reliance on natural ice from New England, for he could import from Old England an artificial refrigerant that used sulfuric acid as a coolant. De Ceta was to do his best to wreck Frederic's business, though in reality he had no way of replicating it himself.

In his efforts to retrieve his right to a monopoly, Frederic had to present a variety of government departments with petitions of various kinds, and was advised by his partner Fellows to oil the wheels of bureaucracy with a few "gratifications." In all, he spent more than two thousand dollars trying to get his monopoly back—all the funds he had managed to scrape together when he had fled Boston. Even so, the island's governing council decided in favor of de Ceta, with the proviso that he backed his claim to be able to supply ice with a bond of thirty thousand dollars. Fancying that he had won the legal battle, de Ceta sailed to Boston and tried to scupper the arrangements for Frederic's first shipment of ice. Like some demon sent to torment Frederic Tudor, he posted advertisements in Boston newspapers claiming that he controlled the ice trade to Havana, and that rivals would have their ships seized if they sailed to Cuba. He wrote to John Russell, the owner of the brig *George Washington*, which was loaded with Frederic's ice and ready to sail, warning him not to leave port and saying he had his own ship prepared.

In Boston, Frederic's younger brother, Harry, had recently become a partner in the ice trade and was looking after shipments. Russell contacted him and was told not to take any notice of de Ceta. At the same time, William Tudor, now no longer concerned with the business, sent Frederic a letter reassuring him that de Ceta was not a real problem, and adding by way of encouragement the news that in order to fund the ice trade Harry had mortgaged Rockwood! If the ice business collapsed, he warned, "Rockwood may be added to your other losses."

However, Frederic was not beaten. He managed to persuade the authorities in Cuba that there should be two years of free trade in ice and that they should allow him to build his icehouse. It was just as well that the entire structure was of portable timbers, because the governor kept changing his mind about where Frederic could erect it. To make the unloading of ice as quick and easy as possible, Frederic naturally wanted the building to be close to the quays. A site was agreed on, and his carpenters set to work on January 27, 1816—two months after they had arrived in Havana. But when he saw the size of the icehouse, the governor said it was too tall. The carpenters took the roof off and lowered the walls by three feet, but it was still too tall. The half-finished structure was then taken down completely, and Frederic had to look for a new site. This proved difficult; those he was offered were too far from the harbor, while those he thought suitable were rejected by the governor. It was not until February 10 that a site was agreed on, and not until three days later that the carpenters were able to start building. All the while, the *George Washington* was sailing southward with its cargo of ice, and was bound to arrive before the new icehouse was finished.

The carpenters had had less than two weeks in which to put up the 159 cedar posts that had been shipped from Boston and that formed the framework of the building, and were still hammering in timber boards and creating the upper story of the icehouse when the *George Washington* docked in Havana on

February 25. Frederic had no choice but to unload the cargo and store it in the unfinished icehouse. Two gangs of black slaves worked for several days carrying the uneven chunks of ice in blankets from ship to shore.

When the first ice went on sale in early March 1816, Frederic noted that it was ten years almost to the day since his first-ever ice sales on the brig *Favorite* in St. Pierre. He had learned a great deal about the business of selling ice in the tropics, but he was still having to improvise, as he had done in Martinique a decade before. Because the icehouse was unfinished and therefore could not be sealed at the top, the ice was melting, a stream of chilly water pouring onto the street.

Frederic measured the rate of loss by collecting meltwater from the icehouse drain in a wooden barrel. At first, he calculated that he was losing fifty-six pounds of ice an hour. This was reduced when the icehouse was finished and the store could be kept shut, but the loss was still too great. Frederic put an extra layer of sawdust, now his favored insulation material, on the outside of the structure, held in place by tin sheeting. This failed because the tin heated up in the sun, spoiling the insulating effect of the sawdust. He then tried replacing the sawdust on top of the ice with blankets. This worked much better, and the ice loss fell to only eighteen pounds an hour. Frederic made these accurate measurements by standing beside the barrel that collected the meltwater and timing the rate at which it filled up.

The Havana icehouse was one of the keys to Frederic's business. Sadly, no pictures of it, nor any plans or illustrations of any kind, have ever been found. We know that it was made of timber and that the outer walls were twenty-five feet long and twenty-five feet high. Inside was the ice store itself, the walls of which were nineteen feet long and sixteen feet high. An upper floor was built over the ice, with a trapdoor down to it from a salesroom that was reached by an outside staircase. Next to the salesroom was another room to provide accommodation when necessary for the icehouse keeper. Insulation was provided by sawdust and peat packed between the inner and outer walls of the store. A drain took the meltwater away.

The most significant aspect of the Havana icehouse was that it was built entirely aboveground, from relatively cheap materials. It was quite unlike the traditional subterranean icehouse, lined with brick or stone and topped with a stone structure, yet it was just as efficient at preserving ice. We do not know quite how Frederic arrived at his design, but the possibility of building aboveground had been in his mind for a long time. As early as 1806, he mentions in a business proposal that he had never seen an icehouse aboveground himself, but that his brother William had taken a look at one in Philadelphia that seemed to keep ice very well. The fact that ice could be preserved in the holds of ships was evidence that it did not need to be stored underground. Some farmers in Virginia had simple, cheap icehouses that caught the attention of the English writer on rural economy William Cobbett, who was traveling in America around the time Frederic was building his icehouse in Havana. Cobbett did not imagine that there was much need for these Virginia icehouses in England, where ice was chiefly used for skating on. However, he included in his *Rural Economy*, published in 1821, instructions on how to build one, on the grounds that "If people must have ice in summer they may as well go a right way as a wrong way about it." He was scornful about the elaborate icehouses built at great cost in England, and provided illustrations for anyone wanting to put up a much simpler and more effective structure.

> Ice will not melt in the hottest sun so soon as in a close and damp cellar. Put a lump of ice in cold water, and one of the same size before a hot fire, and the former will dissolve in half the time the latter will. Let me take this occasion of observing, that an ice-house should never be under ground, or under the shade of trees. That the bed of it ought to be three feet above the level of the ground, that this bed ought to consist of something that will admit the drippings to go instantly off, and the house should stand in a place open to the sun and air. This is the way they have the ice-houses under the burning sun of Virginia; here they keep their fish and meat as fresh and sweet as in winter, when at the same time neither will keep for twelve hours, though let down to the depth of a hundred feet in a well. A Virginian, with some poles and straw, will stick up an ice-house for ten dollars, worth a dozen of those ice-houses, each of which costs our men of taste as many scores of pounds.

The technology of icehouses was the subject of much debate throughout the nineteenth century. There was no way of preventing ice from melting once the air temperature rose above freezing; it was a matter of finding how best to slow down the inevitable thaw. It was not enough to protect the ice from the warm air around it, for the interior of an icehouse has a complex atmosphere of its own. As ice melts, it releases latent heat, which creates a warm and therefore rising draft of air—it was a surprising observation that icehouses could "heat up." In fact, the domes built above traditional icehouses were not merely ornaments, they provided ventilation and allowed this hot air to dissipate. On the other hand, air is a poorer conductor of heat than water, and icehouses had to have effective drains to siphon off the meltwater that would otherwise accumulate and rot the ice from the bottom.

If an insulating material was used in an icehouse, it could easily become damp and heat up at the same time, so that it would give off a nasty smell of carbonic acid. Hay was especially susceptible. Cobbett believed that straw, as used by the Virginians, was the best material, and that nothing else was needed because out in the open it remained dry and therefore sound insulation. He believed that icehouses should not be built of timber, as they would not be airtight, and the wood itself would become damp. Frederic Tudor's Havana icehouse, which was to be the prototype for those constructed all over America later in the century, proved Cobbett wrong. It was timber built with a cavity wall, the space between the inner and outer shells filled with sawdust and peat that remained dry and let in no air. What is not clear is how Frederic ventilated his icehouse, though his diaries show that he had known how important this was for a long time.

Frederic's rival de Ceta appears to have given up his challenge, and soon disappeared from Boston. His claim to be able to make ice artificially proved to be worthless: there were chemical coolant mixtures on sale at the time, but they were no more than a means of chilling wine and other drinks. They could not make ice, and their use of sulfuric acid made them hazardous. Frederic had told the Spanish authorities in Havana that de Ceta was talking rubbish, and that the idea of making ice artificially was "absurd." It never seems to have occurred to him that someone might find a way of undermining his trade by manufacturing ice or making an artificial refrigerator. There had recently been attempts to do so, but none looked likely to challenge the productivity of a New England winter.

Natural freezing occurs when the body of water in a lake or a river reaches a temperature of forty degrees Fahrenheit and the air temperature at the surface stays at thirty-two degrees or below for several hours. A slight movement on the surface of the water begins the formation of crystals, and the ice thickens as long as the air temperature remains below freezing. Left alone, a pond will rarely freeze to a depth of more than two feet. However, Frederic discovered that if holes were drilled in the surface to allow water to well up from below, it would freeze quickly and thicken the ice. This practice became known as "sinking the pond."

There were no simple techniques for replicating the process of natural freezing. It had been known for centuries that the evaporation of liquids, including water, required heat and therefore produced cold. Liquid put in porous earthenware pots could be cooled by evaporation—this was the only ice available to the British in India until the first Yankee ships brought supplies from New England in the 1830s. To produce cold artificially involved the evaporation of gases in elaborately constructed pieces of machinery, and it would take many years of experimentation to arrive at commercially viable plants. At the time Frederic was selling ice in Havana, the potential market for ice and refrigeration was unknown, and until its value for preserving food was proved, and a taste for cool drinks and ice cream was acquired by large numbers of people, there was no commercial incentive to invest in artificial refrigeration. There was not much incentive either to go to the trouble of cutting and shipping natural ice. It was only the obsessive pursuit of the enterprise by Frederic Tudor, and the fact that Boston shippers found ice useful as salable ballast, that kept the frozen-water trade going in its first years. And it was the extensive use of natural ice in America, and to a lesser extent in Europe, that eventually stimulated the development of artificial refrigeration.

But in 1816, there was very little use of ice by tradesmen or farmers, and inventions such as the Maryland engineer Thomas Moore's patent refrigerator, first advertised in 1803, remained a novelty. These insulated iceboxes had very little value before the extensive harvesting and storing of ice provided a regular and reliable supply, as they had to be refilled daily in summer. If people did not have refrigerators or ice stores of some kind, they would not buy ice, therefore it was not worth harvesting it; and if it was not harvested in any quantity, there was no supply. It was the same vicious cycle as there would be in the early days of radio—there was no point in broadcasting if nobody had a wireless set, and it was not worth having one unless there were broadcasts.

At first, Frederic's sales in Havana were slow, partly because the weather was not all that hot. To stimulate trade, he tried to generate rivalry between coffee-shop owners by offering one, and then another, his newly invented water-cooling jar, described in a note in his diary from March 1816: "It consists of a jar of about 14 gallons suspended by ropes and surrounded with one thickness of dry sawdust two inches thick and another of dry moss of the same thickness with two covers one below the other with blanket and a crane with a cock to it to draw off the water."

It is just about possible to imagine what this cunning contraption looked like and how it was supposed to work. It seems to have been designed to enable Frederic to sell the meltwater from the icehouse at a small profit, for it could not actually cool anything—it would simply keep water cold long enough for it to be sold by the glass. Nevertheless, Frederic had high hopes for it, noting in his diary: "Drink Spaniards and be cool that I, who have suffered so much in the cause, may be able to go home and keep myself warm." Some coffee-shop owners gave it a try, but the novelty soon wore off, and the chief trade in ice continued to be for the making of ice cream.

Supplies of ice were now being shipped to Cuba throughout the summer. It had been stored in icehouses on the shores of ponds close to Boston as soon as it was cut in winter, and could be taken out as necessary. Sales began to pick up, and with his icehouse functioning efficiently, Frederic began a new experiment, this time in the preservation of fruit. A fresh cargo of ice was about to leave Boston, and he asked for some Baldwin apples to be packed in barrels and buried in the hold alongside the ice. They arrived after a month at sea in good condition, with only a few bad apples in each barrel, and Frederic sold them at a profit. Encouraged by this, he wondered if he might not turn a profit selling tropical fruit from Cuba in America. To test the feasibility of this, he had two boxes of oranges stored in the icehouse, one buried in straw in the ice and the other put above the ice. After a month only one orange had gone bad in the box placed on top of the ice, and Frederic felt this was proof enough that he could ship Cuban produce to America for a good return.

In August 1816, the schooner *Parago* arrived in Havana with a cargo of ice, giving Frederic the chance to pioneer the shipment of Cuban fruit to New York. He was so confident of success that he borrowed three thousand dollars in Havana at an interest rate of 40 percent so he could buy a full cargo of fruit and pay the freight to New York. He left fifteen tons of ice in the hold of the schooner and packed in with it a consignment of limes, oranges, plantains, bananas, coconuts, and pears. On top of this, he laid about three tons of hay as insulation. As his cousin William Savage was now back in Cuba, he left him in charge of ice sales and sailed with his cargo on the *Parago*. It was the hottest time of the year, and the schooner set off under a burning sun. The hold heated up and began to belch steam, and the wet hay became so warm there was a fear that the whole ship might spontaneously combust. This anxiety lasted until the *Parago* sailed into cooler waters and Frederic's tropical cargo simmered down. They docked in New York on September 17, and the fruit was examined. A very large part of it had simply rotted away in the steambath of the first few days of the voyage. Frederic believed he had packed too much fruit in too little ice. Most of the limes and about a third of the oranges were salable, but the price they fetched was disappointing, partly because they had arrived in the height of the season for locally grown produce.

In all, Frederic lost about two thousand dollars on the

Parago venture, wiping out the small profits he had made from ice sales in Havana. He was falling ever deeper in debt. It was at this very low point that his elder brother William offered a ray of hope. He had written Frederic an encouraging letter, saying that people in Boston now had a real regard for the ice business, and that there was a possible new market to try. An old friend of their father, General Thomas Pinckney, had been visiting Boston. Pinckney had served as a major-general in the War of 1812, had been governor of South Carolina, and was the owner of a very large plantation with more than two hundred slaves. William had suggested to him that he might be interested in the rather unusual trade his younger brother Frederic was pursuing. Pinckney expressed some enthusiasm, and said Frederic should write to him with an account of how an ice trade with South Carolina might become established. Frederic immediately sent Pinckney a proposal, then returned to Boston full of anxiety, as there was a good chance he would be met by a sheriff with a warrant for his arrest.

He did not stay long in Boston. There was a letter waiting from General Pinckney saying that he and a young relative would consider backing the importation of ice to South Carolina. As he had no money, Frederic did not know how to pursue this possibility. His elder brother William had nothing to invest either, having spent the duration of the War of 1812 in England involved in a business with some friends who had opened a factory making nails, which was a failure. However, Frederic now had a piece of luck. He mentioned Pinckney's offer to a friend, Francis Lee, who was from a family of successful Boston merchants. Lee thought Frederic should go to

Charleston right away, and when Frederic said he could not afford to, Lee loaned him three hundred dollars. Charleston was a boomtown, profiting from the demand for American cotton, and Lee clearly thought there was a good chance that it would be a profitable market for New England ice.

With a new debt, Frederic sailed for Charleston on November 1, 1816, knowing that the sheriffs were pursuing him for repayment of four loans. He was the only member of the family with any prospect of saving Rockwood and restoring the Tudors' former wealth, and the only trade that seemed to have any chance of succeeding was the export of ice.

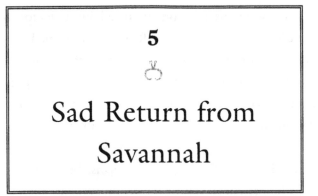

5

Sad Return from
Savannah

It took Frederic's ship the *Milo* just a week to reach
Charleston; if he opened up a market for ice here, it would
be much easier to supply than Havana or St. Pierre. He had
a new scheme for establishing the trade: instead of seeking a
monopoly from the state of South Carolina, he would raise
between five and ten thousand dollars through subscription to
build a large icehouse and put ice on the market at a low price.
He circulated a letter with this proposal. Charles Cotesworth
Pinckney, nephew of General Pinckney and prospective partner
in the South Carolina ice venture, introduced Frederic to a
lawyer, Langdon Cheves, who had excellent connections to the
leading politicians of the state.

Cheves persuaded Frederic to stick to his customary tactic
of seeking a monopoly for the supply of ice, and had already
arranged for a petition to be put to the legislature. Frederic

agreed, and with his petition endorsed by a doctor and the Charleston City Council, sent off his application. From bitter experience, however, he knew that this might be an expensive waste of time, and decided to hedge his bets. He approached a Boston merchant, Samuel Davenport, who was in business in Charleston, and proposed that if he put up the money for an icehouse he could have a one-third interest in the business. They could not at first agree on terms, because Davenport wanted a bigger cut in return for his investment, but a deal was done provided Frederic was granted a monopoly.

The South Carolina legislature was in the state capital, Columbia, and Frederic was advised to go there in support of his petition. He reluctantly agreed. It took him three days to reach the town, a miserable journey over rough roads, and he fell ill. After several days in bed, he presented himself to the committee, which heard his petition, and Frederic found them generally unsympathetic. It had nothing to do with their lack of enthusiasm for Boston ice; it was the issue of the monopoly that caused a political rift in the committee. Frederic lost his temper, stormed out without waiting for the inevitable rejection, and went straight back to Charleston, determined to get the business started anyway. Ignoring the fact that without a monopoly he had no deal with Davenport, he wrote to his chief ice supplier in Boston to arrange for four carpenters to come to Charleston and start work on an icehouse.

It was now early 1817. The Judge had written to Frederic that seeking monopolies in the United States of America was a waste of time:

All that any Legislature of a free and commercial State ought to grant in a Case like yours should be a Bonus or Premium for a year or two, to introduce the Luxury you proffer them. What has the Majority of the Citizens to gain from the Introduction of an article that can never reach them? The wealthy ones of Charleston and its Invirons [sic] alone can enjoy the pleasant Effect and are able to pay for their exclusive Benefits.

The refusal of the monopoly in Charleston was, as it turned out, the least of Frederic's problems. He managed to persuade Davenport to back him anyway, and construction of a large icehouse similar to that in Havana was begun. Frederic did not agree with his father that the only customers would be the very wealthy. He had moved on from the belief that this was simply a "luxury" trade. If he kept the price reasonably low, he believed the habit of using ice would catch on and become a routine part of everyday life in Charleston during the summer months. It was this first Charleston venture that really began the American ice trade, which was to grow into a huge industry later in the century, for it included nearly all the elements that made that possible.

When the icehouse was ready that summer, Frederic was able to fill it right away with a consignment from Boston that had been harvested the previous winter and then stored. He put an advertisement in a Charleston newspaper that is worth quoting in full; he kept a copy pasted in his icehouse diaries:

The Ice establishment at Fitzsimon's wharf is now opened. Ice will be for sale at all hours of the day, from sunrise to sundown, except when the Ice House Keeper is necessarily absent at his meals. It will be sold in any quantity from one pound to 500 pounds. The Ice House will be open a few hours on Sunday morning. The price will be eight and a third cents a pound with an allowance of four per centum to those who purchase largely or by tickets. The price at which it is now offered in Charleston is as low as it was in the northern cities when the article was first introduced in them in the summer season; and when it is remembered that the capital invested in this undertaking falls very little short of $10,000 and the very great waste which must necessarily take place in the best constructed icehouse it must be apparent that the profit cannot be more than reasonable however great the consumption may be. The inhabitants therefore are invited to call for ice in such quantities as shall enable the proprietor of the house to continue the present price which cannot be the case unless ice is used rather *as a necessary of life than as a luxury*.

The best method of carrying ice in a small quantity is to wrap it in a blanket. These may be had at the ice-house of sufficient size at $1. Of the mode of keeping ice best when it is carried home it is to be observed that it should be kept in that part of the house which is least cool, that is to say in a dry closet where there is no circulation of air . . . it is a well attested principle that whatever will keep a man warm, with the exception of the sun and fire, will keep ice cold.

A family could get a regular supply of Tudor ice for ten dollars a month, and Frederic urged the people of Charleston to buy tickets for this ice in advance. The reason: "There have been instances where negroes have been detected in holding back one half of the money sent and attributing the small quantity of ice returned to its thawing on the way."

Later that year, Frederic began for the first time to sell domestic refrigerators made in Boston and shipped to Charleston.

The steely determination of Frederic Tudor to overcome all misadventures is captured in this portrait of the Boston "Ice King." He was slightly built, weighing only around 130 pounds, but was full of energy.

OVERLEAF *Left* The first entry in Tudor's Ice House Diary, which he began on August 5, 1805: "William & myself have this day determined to get together what property we have & embark in the undertaking of carrying ice to the West Indies the ensuing winter." The first cargo was sold in Martinique the following March.

Right The cover of Tudor's first diary, kept in a leather-bound farmer's almanac. The inscription reads: "He who gives back at first repulse and without striking the second blow, despairs of success, has never been, is not, and never will be, a hero in war, love or business." That was his credo.

Plan &c. of transporting Ice to
Tropical climates.

Boston Aug.st 1st 1805. _ William & myself have
this day determined to get together what of what
we have & could collect _ a cargo of [a] ship of
ice to the west Indies the ensuing [winter].

Aug. 12th. that of my [time] & [behalf] with
Samuel [Savage] to Niagara Falls which
we returned about 2d Oct. to now proceed
with William in furthering our scheme
_ We [find] the [want] of some person
to take a part in it _ not only to bear
his proportion of the expenses but to [advise]
with us [as] to [measures] to be adopted _
for this purpose I wrote the following
letter to Wm Otis _ which is the outline of
our project.

Sir I live in a country where at some
seasons of the year the heat is almost
insupportable & where at times those
comforts [or necessary] of life & water cannot
be had but in a tepid state _ Ice must
be considered as outweighing most other
luxuries.

However absurd Sir the Idea
may at first appear that ice can be
transported to tropical climates & preserved
there during the most intemperate
heats yet for the following reasons it
does appear to me certain that the thing

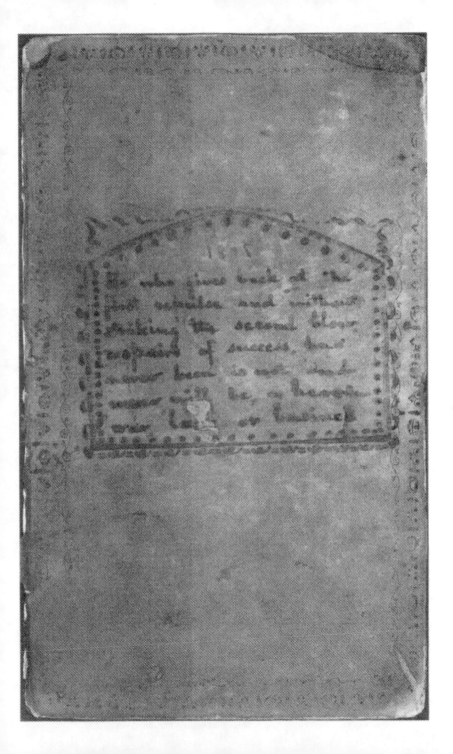

He who gives back at the first repulse and without striking the second blow despairs of success, has never been, is not and never will be, a hero in war, love or business.

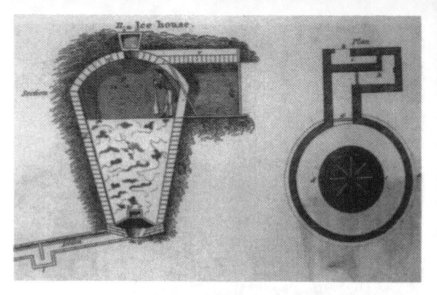

A design for the kind of ice-house built for the aristocracy in Europe and America in the early nineteenth century. The melt-water is drained away and there is a dome above the pit for the circulation of air. It was the belief then that harvested ice kept best underground in a shady place.

An 1845 advertisement for the Fresh Pond Hotel in Cambridge, Massachusetts, which in summer was a popular resort for Harvard students who fished and swam in its clear water. Most winters it froze to a depth of more than a foot, and the ice cut here was exported to India.

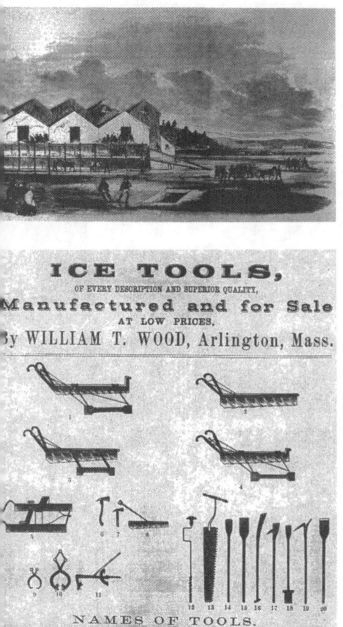

An 1830 lithograph of ice harvesters at work on Fresh Pond. It was here in 1827 that the manager of the Fresh Pond Hotel, Nathaniel Wyeth, invented the horse-drawn ice plough for cutting regular blocks. These were hauled up into the stores by a pulley system powered by harnessed horses. Sawdust was the favorite insulating material.

As ice harvesting became big business a range of special-ized tools was devised for cutting, moving, and storing huge blocks. The ploughs shown here were drawn by one or two horses.

ICE TOOLS,

OF EVERY DESCRIPTION AND SUPERIOR QUALITY,

Manufactured and for Sale

AT LOW PRICES,

By WILLIAM T. WOOD, Arlington, Mass.

NAMES OF TOOLS.

No. 1, Swing Guide Marker, full size. No. 2, Cast steel Plow, from 6 to 14 inches deep. No. 3, Stationary Guide Plow. No. 4, Swing Guide Plow, from 4 to 8 inches deep. No. 5, Snow-Ice Plane. No. 6, Ice Axe. No. 7, Chest Hatchet. No. 8, Hand Plow. No. 9, Hand Tongs, loading, medium, small and family sizes. No. 10, Hoisting Tongs. No. 11, Grapple. No. 12, Auger. No. 13, Saw. No. 14, Splitting Chisel. No. 15, Caulking Bar. No. 16, Starting Chisel. No. 17, Hook Chisel. No. 18, Breaking Bar. No. 19, Ice Hook. No. 20, Bar or Packing Chisel.

W. & S. HOWE, Printers, 22 Merchants Row, Boston.

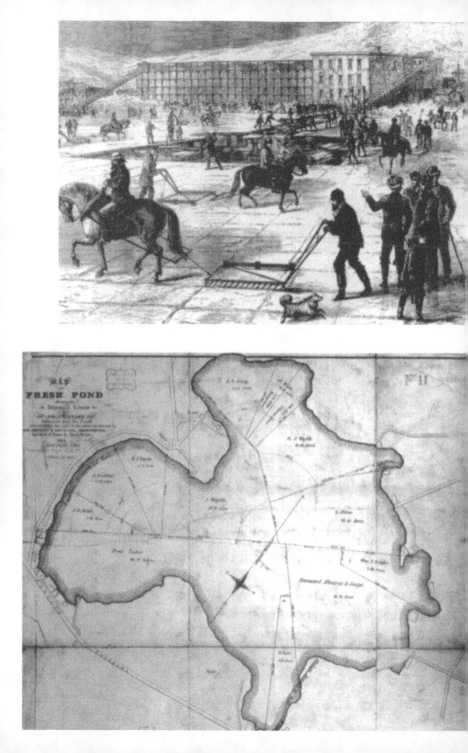

OPPOSITE *Above* The spectacle of ice harvesting often drew interested crowds in fine weather. This illustration is of ploughing and storing ice on the Hudson River, New York. It shows the ice ploughs being pulled by mounted horses, which was not the usual practice, and may be the result of a lapse of memory by the artist. But the scale of the operation is not fanciful.

Below As more and more companies began to harvest ice from Fresh Pond, a Harvard law professor, Simon Greenleaf, was asked to devise a scheme to establish ownership. He decided the amount of ice allowed should be directly related to the length of shoreline owned. In 1841 a surveyor drew up this map, on a scale of two hundred feet to the inch. It shows that Tudor and Wyeth had the lion's share of the

Left The inscription on this trophy reads: "Presented by Lord William Bentinck, Governor-General & Commander-in-Chief, India to Mr. Rogers of Boston in Acknowledgment of the Spirit and enterprise which projected and successfully executed the first attempt to import a cargo of American ice into Calcutta. Nov. 22nd 1833." Rogers, as Tudor's business partner, traveled with the ice to India, then disappeared along with the cup. It turned up in the 1980s and is now in the Peabody Essex Museum in Salem, Massachusetts.

Below The British in India regarded American ice as a great luxury, and some had refrigerators like this one, dating from 1872, to cool their drinks. They also adopted the American habit of putting lumps of lake ice in their drinks, though this never caught on in Victorian England.

Ships at the Tudor Wharves in Charlestown harbor, Boston, loading ice which would be exported to India, Cuba, New Orleans, and sometimes round Cape Horn to San Francisco. Ice blocks stored in these insulated warehouses would melt slowly enough to provide stocks all through the summer.

The magnificent ice-house built by the British on the seafront in Madras in the 1830s. As Madras has no harbor, the blocks of ice had to be unloaded into small boats and carried over the surf. Four bearers were needed to carry each block, which was protected from the sun by a cloth until it was stored in the ice-house.

These "Little Ice Houses" were made to his own design and were probably similar to those invented for farmers by Thomas Moore fourteen years earlier. There is no record of what they looked like, but they would have been wooden boxes with insulation and an inner lining of metal, probably iron. They were made to hold a daily allowance of three pounds of ice, which would chill drinks, be used for ice cream making, and preserve fresh fruit.

The Charleston venture was a considerable success, but the one in Havana in the meantime had suffered a series of disasters. While he was setting up the South Carolina business, Frederic received a letter from his partner Nathaniel Fellows saying the authorities had given orders for the Havana icehouse to be taken down, and asking what he should do with the dismantled structure. The agent for supplying Boston ice to Cuba wanted his bills paid. Frederic's younger brother, Harry, who until that time had lived an adventurous but dissolute life, wrote to say he was being sued and asked Frederic to bail him out. Frederic wrote back in April 1817: "I thought for a moment I must sell my watch and escape home—abandon my Havana business, this [i.e., Charleston] also and sink into utter despair." He added, however: "I put my shoulder to the wheel and after many a hard struggle I have rolled my wagon on."

Though he had hoped to stay in Charleston to get the trade established there, Frederic felt he had to go to Havana to sort out the matter of the icehouse. David Day, the icehouse keeper, had died the previous February, and Frederic sent a carpenter, Joshua Marston, to take temporary charge. When he himself sailed for Cuba on the schooner *Martha* on May 20, he was ready to abandon Havana altogether and to concentrate on the American market. Social life was much pleasanter in Charleston, where he had been accepted into the top tier of the plantation world because of his family contacts and the tremendous appreciation for his promise to deliver regular supplies of ice. When he reached Havana, he discovered that Joshua Marston had died of yellow fever, which had reached epidemic proportions. Two other carpenters he had sent later had sailed back to Boston as soon as they learned that the fever was rampant. However, the icehouse had not been torn down, and still held a good quantity of ice. Frederic's Havana partner, Nathaniel Fellows, refused to buy the business, but agreed to take it on provided Frederic kept an interest in it. Frederic therefore found a new icehouse keeper and got the trade going again.

Once that was settled, Frederic made plans to open up a new market in Savannah, Georgia, not far south of Charleston. He could not wait to leave Havana, and feared every day that he would come down with yellow fever. This time, unlike in 1910, he was lucky, and made his escape in good health on June 19, taking a ship straight to Savannah. He found there was interest in his ice there, but in summer the wealthier residents all left the city, and he was unable to raise a large enough subscription to build an icehouse. He went back to Charleston, where he enjoyed the social round until yellow fever broke out and he sailed on again, this time to Philadelphia, where he hoped to discuss with the Portuguese minister there the prospect of sending ice to Rio de Janeiro. He had no luck, as there was a rebellion in Brazil, so in August he sailed to New York, where he paused to take stock of his position. He had begun to realize that his best markets were likely to be Charleston, Savannah, and possibly New Orleans. But he had no money, and a return to Boston would almost certainly land him in jail, for he had escaped the sheriffs too often and owed too much.

From New York, Frederic wrote to Fellows in Havana: "I am afraid to go home . . . I beg you to consider the urgency of my situation." The Cuban ice business that he had previously tried to jettison offered the only prospect for immediate funds, and he hoped Fellows would oblige. In the meantime, he decided that he needed a break from the ice trade altogether, and took a boat to Cape Cod. He still had a lease on land there and on Martha's Vineyard for the coal-mining venture that had been abandoned for lack of funds. In Sandwich, Cape Cod, he met up with a group of people on a jaunt from Boston and stayed with them for two weeks.

Frederic had been brought up in a prosperous Boston family that was now almost destitute, his grandfather's estate spent or mortgaged, his father, for whom he felt great affection, humiliated by debt and surviving in an unfashionable district of Boston on a meager salary. His sister Delia had been forced into a disastrous marriage, for which he himself was largely responsible, and her husband, Charles Stewart, now doing very well in the world, would not help him. He had fallen out with his older brother William, who had no money nor any inclination, it seemed, to acquire any: he was pursuing a literary career in Boston editing the *North American Review*.

His younger brother, Harry, was a billiard-playing, brandy-drinking wastrel. Frederic had wanted him to come to Cape Cod, but Harry did not turn up. The family had more or less fallen apart.

Frederic had few friends, and quite a few enemies. He searched for people he could trust to help run his ice business, but they continually let him down, or died, or tried to take more than their fair share of the profits. On Cape Cod, wondering what his next move should be, he was close to giving in to despair. The tantalizing truth was that he was very close to the breakthrough he needed, which was one decent season selling ice at a profit without any more disasters. He had a constellation of carpenters, agents, suppliers, and icehouse keepers now, so the business could run itself provided everyone behaved honestly. The industry he had invented worked, and if he was not careful, someone else not weighed down as he was with debt would take it from him. He evidently had quite a few rivals by now, for he notes how he beat them off by lowering the price of his ice until the opposition gave in. It would be interesting to know who his competitors were, but Frederic's diaries do not attach names to them, and we can only assume that they were shippers taking ice as ballast without any plans to establish a regular industry.

In October 1817, Frederic returned briefly to Boston, then sailed for New York, noting that he was once again obliged to leave "in the manner of an escape." But he had collected some money sent from Havana by his partner Fellows, and his short holiday appears to have given him a new optimism. As he was in any case on the run from his creditors, he decided not to use the

Havana profits to pay off any debts, but to start a new business in Savannah. From New York he sailed on to Charleston, where ice sales had gone well despite the outbreak of yellow fever, which had driven many potential customers out of town. Charleston had become Frederic's favorite refuge: he liked the town and its people, and they liked his ice. That autumn he went on to Savannah, where he was not so well received, and could find little interest in his subscription scheme. He went back to Charleston to spend the winter.

Now, not for the first or the last time, the New England weather threatened to destroy the ice trade altogether. In December 1817, Frederic wrote in his diary the admonition that he later inscribed on the cover of his first-ever icehouse diary, begun in 1805: "He who gives back at first repulse and without striking the second blow, despairs of success, has never been, is not, and never will be, a hero in love, war or business." He had already struck many second blows and now faced another test of his resolve, for there was precious little ice to be had on Fresh Pond or anywhere else in Massachusetts. Every few years, there would be an exceptionally warm winter, and this was one of them. Frederic's suppliers did manage to harvest enough for a cargo that went out on the *Luna*, but four days out of Boston, the ship was dismasted and spent forty-six days at sea before making shore, but not at Havana. A second cargo was sent on the *Cicero,* which was wrecked. There would be no profits from Havana, and the ice would run out that summer.

Frederic's continuous traveling had made it impossible to keep his diaries up to date, and the entries are scattered. There is one written around this time, however, that sets out his circum-stances exactly:

> Had you not better entirely abandon this ice business? It is a subject which wears out body and mind while it pre-vents you from having the standing among your fellow men which you deserve. It occupies all your attention and appears at best subject to great hazard. In the course of twelve years pursuit you have arrived at little certainty and there can be little doubt that the exertions which you have made in this business would have given you better situation and the confidence of others which you are now without. You stand at best a well-intentioned schemer and projector when you might, with a more regular application to common mercantile business, become a more useful and respected member of society. It is not too late, you are not yet 36 years old and you may yet get back into the old road. Sell out in the best way you can and become a regular man.
>
> Answer: The suggestions of doubt are too late . . . My reputation is now so far pledged that I must advance, and should I be able to secure Savannah and New Orleans I am tolerably certain of doing very handsomely. I, therefore, throw away every discouraging thought and determine to push on with as much exertion as I can command and en-deavour to deserve success.

There was, in fact, just enough profit from Charleston that year to fund another attempt to get the trade going in Savannah. To test the market, Frederic managed to get some ice shipped even in that unproductive winter, though there was no purpose-built icehouse in Savannah, then went back to Boston when the tropical heat of summer made Charleston less pleasant and there was once again the danger of yellow fever. He managed to survive the summer and autumn without being sent to jail, and in December, with another winter and another harvest on its way, sailed to Savannah with the idea of building an icehouse there.

Perhaps because the booming cotton town had begun to put up brick buildings to replace its mostly wooden structures, Frederic decided he would build his first brick icehouse. By January 1819, it was taking shape, with thirty workmen under Frederic's supervision creating a store with a capacity of twelve to thirteen thousand square feet, which could hold more than two hundred tons of ice—enough, as he put it, to "keep all Georgia cool for some time." The insulation in the cavity walls was pulverized charcoal.

The regular Savannah trade began in February 1819, with a cargo of 160 tons. Though Frederic did not like Savannah, he was greatly encouraged by the enthusiasm its inhabitants appeared to have for his ice. Almost immediately the market expanded, for he took orders from inland towns such as Augusta and Darien, which could be reached by riverboat. He actually sold ice more quickly in Savannah than in Charleston. By the spring, he had a new and thriving venture, and was anxious to return to Boston. He left Savannah on July 4, 1819, and wrote as he sailed north: "I leave Savannah with no inconsiderable satisfaction as everything goes with tolerable smoothness. But best of all 'I think I shall when I once more place my foot on land quit it no more.' "

At last, Frederic was going home with good news and some

real reward for his efforts. He had forcefully rejected the advice of his well-meaning brother-in-law Robert Gardiner to abandon his pursuit of wealth and to find other pleasures in life. His father, seeing Frederic driven almost mad by the setbacks he had had to contend with in the ice trade, had said the same. At times, Frederic had been close to accepting the fate that had befallen the Judge, with his failed speculations and overlavish style of living. Though his father had been largely responsible for depriving Frederic and his brothers of the comfortable lifestyle they might have had, there appears to have been no animosity toward him. He was a jovial and endearing character, and they remembered the good times they had had as children.

Frederic may have been driven chiefly by the pursuit of success and wealth, but he also always had in mind rescuing his father from his lowly position and impoverished life. Aboard the brig *Almira* heading back to Boston, he looked forward to telling the Judge how well things were going in Charleston and Savannah, and about his plans to reopen old markets and to take the ice trade farther south, to New Orleans. He did not learn until he arrived in Boston that the Judge had died peacefully on July 8, while Frederic was at sea. He wrote of his father's death in November, confiding in his diary:

> He died without any call to the Physician or trouble to the nurses. He was a little (as was thought) indisposed four days preceding his death and while laying on the bed, conversing with his accustomed hilarity and pleasantry suddenly gasped and expired: dying as he always wished he should without trouble to others or pain to himself.

Frederic added: "He is dead & with him much of what can make life to me agreeable."

That winter, in a solemn mood, Frederic began to plan his next season. He might have expected that for once everything would be straightforward, but the frozen-water trade continued to set him new challenges, and to survive required all the enterprise and ingenuity he could muster.

6

The Crack-Up

Although he had experienced problems in getting ice when he first began the trade with Martinique, and there had been warm winters since that had threatened to cut the amount of his supplies, Frederic was generally confident that, whatever else might go wrong, Nature or God Almighty would manufacture all the frozen water he was ever likely to need. He used to say, "Winter never rots in the sky." The quantities of ice he was shipping were quite small, and he was able to store a good deal in his Boston icehouses to fulfill orders in the summer. The greatest danger was that a cargo would be lost at sea either through shipwreck or a slow voyage.

As well as seeking new markets and hanging on to those already established, Frederic set out to revive those that had been lost. With the exception of Havana, the West Indies trade had petered out. The exclusive privileges his brother William had been granted ten years earlier had now expired, so Frederic sent another envoy to Europe to ask for them to be reinstated. This was Stephen Cabot, member of a wealthy Boston family, for whom some kind of occupation had to be found. Frederic sent Cabot to Europe early in 1817, at the time he himself was setting up the trade with Charleston. The British refused to grant any ice privileges, so Cabot went on to France, where he succeeded in renewing the monopoly for Martinique and Guadeloupe. As the colonial officials there had to endorse these privileges, Cabot sailed for the islands, arriving in March 1818, a year after he had left Boston. He was pleased with himself and anxious to get his first experience of the ice trade that winter, as he had been promised the position of agent on Martinique. This meant, first of all, getting a new icehouse built there. He and his family were therefore deeply disappointed when Frederic told them it was "too early," and they must not rush in—an approach to business that was uncharacteristic of him.

To be involved with Frederic at this time was still to raise eyebrows in Boston, and Cabot keenly felt the snub he had received. He had no money of his own and no job, and asked Frederic to explain his predicament to his friends. Frederic suggested he brazen it out, as he had had to do himself, and adopt a defiant attitude. He noted in his diary: "I put all their opinion at a non plus . . . I walked & bowed & smiled & talked like other men when they feel within them that they stand firm and need neither the assistance, the good wishes or money of anyone."

The real reason Frederic felt unable to send Cabot right off to Martinique was that he could not afford to do so. But then he had a windfall, receiving $5,600 in insurance money for the loss of the two ships that were to have taken ice to Havana the previous year. Shortly afterward, he was sent five thousand dollars by Samuel Davenport, his partner in the Charleston business. This was not quite enough to set up the Martinique business again, but then Frederic managed to persuade an investor to put up another five thousand. Cabot would be able to sail to Martinique after all, taking with him the frame for a timber icehouse and the carpenters to put it together. He left in October 1818, and the icehouse was ready when the first cargo arrived at St. Pierre at the end of March 1819. Sales went well under the new icehouse keeper, John Damon, a well-respected carpenter employed by Frederic. A second cargo was sent out, and Cabot, excited by the success of the Martinique trade, sailed back to Boston to suggest that he might be given a bigger cut of the business.

It was July 1819, and Frederic had just gotten back from Savannah and learned of his father's death. He was in no mood to raise Cabot's pay, and told him so. The dispute was brought to an abrupt end by the news that the thriving Martinique business was about to be dissolved: they had run out of ice. It was midsummer, and there were no stores left in Boston. Where could they get ice in midsummer? There was only one solution—icebergs.

Every spring, great chunks of the Arctic Circle break away from the ice sheet and float southward, creating a hazard to shipping (it was one of these icebergs that in 1912 would sink the *Titanic*). Now and again, a ship's captain had taken the risk of chipping bits off an iceberg to provide his crew with fresh water. For that is what icebergs are, huge chunks of compressed and frozen rainwater that float, nine-tenths submerged, in the saltwater of the sea.

Stephen Cabot managed to find a Captain Hadlock, from the port of Castine, in Maine, who was prepared to sail north in the brig *Retrieve* and track down and hack off a bit of an iceberg near the Labrador coast. The ship left harbor on August 13, and a month later was in the ice floes looking for a good prospect. It was a risky venture—men would have to climb onto the iceberg's treacherous shores and hack bits off, which would then be gathered from the sea by others on the boat. During the first attempts to get in a cargo, a gale blew up, and the men had to leave the iceberg they had carefully chosen and take refuge in a bay. When the storm cleared, they found another iceberg that looked promising and started hacking away at it—but from one side only. This had the effect of causing an imbalance in the floating mass of ice. As they were finishing the job of filling the ship's hold, the iceberg tumbled over, cutting a gash in the side of the ship and threatening to sink it. Vigorous pumping kept it afloat, and Captain Hadlock was able to reach Martinique and earn his fee of $1,700 to relieve the ice famine in the West Indies.

The Martinique business was saved, and Cabot returned to the island. But the profits from St. Pierre appeared to Frederic to be far lower than they should have been. In the belief that the ice trade was booming, Cabot spent freely and got into debt. Reluctantly, Frederic settled his bills and bailed him out. All the while, Cabot was trying to extend the trade, and he persuaded Frederic to invest in a second icehouse on the island of St.

Thomas. Yet no money was being sent back to Boston. Frederic became more and more disillusioned with Cabot, who had fallen in love with a local girl and showed signs of "going native." In frustration, Frederic wrote to him setting out a marketing strategy for ice that he believed would improve sales and bring him some return on his investment. The letter reveals better than any other surviving document Frederic's approach to the frozen-water trade at this time:

> The creams [i.e., ice cream] are the first great object and thereafter cold drinks at the same price as warm . . . A man who has drank [sic] his drinks cold at the same expense for one week can never be presented with them warm again . . . When we have persuaded 100 persons by means of our *same price* plan . . . these 100 will soon carry with them 100 more and that ratio will compound faster than we can calculate.

One way of promoting cold drinks was to offer bartenders free ice and persuade them to serve customers cold drinks at the same price as those that were unchilled. This is what Frederic had done in Havana with his cooler jar. In the manner of a drug pusher, he set out to create a taste for cold that would get customers hooked. As Cabot appeared unconvinced, and wanted to continue to sell the luxury of chilled drinks at a premium, Frederic gave him a more recent example of how, in practice, his method of pushing ice worked. In Charleston, he had stayed in a boardinghouse run by a Mrs. Woodrouff, whose guests ate at a communal table. He made up a cooler jar to hold iced water and had it placed at his side at mealtimes. "This was the subject of ridicule to the household *everyone* of the boarders declared they would not touch the water & endanger their health," Frederic wrote to Cabot. "As I calculated how long their resolution would last, I had the jar made to contain 4 gallons. I found that the high resolution and firm determination was soon overcome without any persuasion of mine & that after a time every man drank the water *no other* and that 4 gallons was not enough."

Frederic was now committed to a policy of persuading all sections of society to enjoy iced drinks, and claimed that in Savannah even the plantation slaves had acquired a taste for them. Of the six thousand dollars' worth of ice he had sold there in 1820 only one thousand dollars' worth was bought by the rich, with the rest going to tradesmen such as butchers and dairymen, to preserve their produce, and to lowlier customers.

It is not clear what Cabot was up to on Martinique, or why he ignored all Frederic's advice and pressed for a new icehouse to be built on St. Thomas, and another on Guadeloupe. But the profits Frederic was making in Charleston and Savannah were draining away in the Cabot venture—Frederic's pursuit of an old market was heading for disaster.

There was, however, a new and potentially huge market for ice in New Orleans. Attempts had been made by others to set up the trade there as early as 1809, and Frederic was aware of a more recent and concerted venture that threatened to head him off in Louisiana. A man named Richard Salmon had built an icehouse in New Orleans, and in 1818 was shipping ice there from Boston. He had copied the Tudor methods closely, and was even selling refrigerators that he called "cellerettes." But he had little capital, and soon ran out of money. In December 1819, when Frederic was planning his move on New Orleans, Salmon, already bankrupt, died of yellow fever. The way was open for Frederic, but he now had no money himself. He estimated that Cabot's West Indian enterprise had cost him almost nineteen thousand dollars and had shown little or no profit. The whole business was closed down in 1821, and Cabot ended up living in Haiti with his Martinique lover, whom local laws forbade him to marry. He died ten years later, branded by Frederic an "unfortunate schemer."

New Orleans was a mouthwatering prospect for Frederic. A great trading post on the Mississippi in the sweltering heat of Louisiana and with a reputation for wild living, it was on a well-established sea route through the Gulf of Mexico and a hundred miles into the delta—but Frederic had no means of reaching it. When he was setting up the Charleston and Savannah trade, he had discussed moving on to New Orleans with a prospective partner he met in New York, but the two fell out and the project came to nothing. Frederic feared that this partner, having learned the details of the trade, was planning to go it alone. This did not happen, but then Richard Salmon appeared and it seemed certain that someone was going to take this valuable market away unless Frederic got in there quickly.

Salvation could not have come from two less promising sources—his brothers William and Harry. Frederic had raised about two thousand dollars, but still needed another three thousand to fund the shipping and building of an icehouse in New Orleans. By September 1820, he had given up hope of getting anything established that winter. He noted in his diary on the twenty-fifth:

> I shall now set out to trim my vessel, adjust the sails &
> regulate the ballast, economize & bring to perfection those
> concerns which are already established & rest satisfied on
> the subject of New Orleans with having attempted every-
> thing which could be possibly thought of & having failed.

At this point, his elder brother William, editing the *North American Review* and enjoying the life of an essayist of some reputation, called to see Frederic in his Boston office, or "counting
room." Naturally, Frederic imagined that William, who was
largely dependent on him, wanted money. He did, but it would
involve a deal that would give Frederic the last piece of capital
he needed to set up in New Orleans. William had some friends
and admirers in Boston who were anxious that he should continue what they saw as a promising literary career. These benefactors would be prepared to invest in Frederic's New Orleans
venture if, in return, he promised to provide William with an
annuity of six hundred dollars a year, which would come in part
from the profits of the enterprise. Frederic could hardly believe
his luck. He quickly agreed to the proposal and drew up the
necessary papers, which secured him two thousand dollars. His
brother-in-law Robert Gardiner then offered to help, and Frederic accepted a further one thousand from him.

Only a month after he had given up hope on New Orleans,
he had set carpenters to work on the timber frame for an icehouse there. What he needed now was an agent. His younger
brother Harry would not in normal circumstances have been a
contender for the post, but Frederic needed to move quickly.
Since his first and hopeless experience in Jamaica, Harry had

enjoyed a few adventures. His brother-in-law, the sea captain Charles Stewart, had found him a sinecure on his ship, on which he had spent two years touring the Mediterranean and England. The pretense had been that Harry, with no suitable qualifications, would act as "judge advocate" on the ship. In fact, he had nothing to do, and simply enjoyed the voyage. Harry had been back in Boston for some time, and had been given the task of looking after the farm at Rockwood. Frederic was furious with him for felling one of his favorite trees for the paltry value of its timber, and it was quite clear that Harry had no more chance of making Rockwood pay than any other Tudor. He also owed eight hundred dollars, and was in danger of being imprisoned for debt. The only solution was to send him to New Orleans. Frederic provided surety for Harry's debts—he would not have been given permission to leave Boston otherwise—and offered to pay him five hundred dollars to run the business for the first season.

On November 9, 1820, Harry was on his way to New Orleans with orders to find a site for the icehouse so that when the materials arrived, work on its construction could begin right away. The length of the voyage was unpredictable, but it was expected to take no longer than five or six weeks. Ten days after Harry left, the *Phoenix* followed, loaded with timber for the icehouse and carpenters to put it together. Provided winter did not "rot in the sky," Frederic should be delivering ice to New Orleans the following March, and he reckoned that if they could sell ten dollars' worth a day, they would be in business.

As always, events took an unexpected turn. Harry made good time to New Orleans, but found that prospective backers there had pulled out, leaving him short of funds. Frederic's two prodigal brothers had gotten him this far; now it was his father's turn to come to his aid from beyond the grave. Twenty years earlier, when the Judge was enjoying his inheritance, he had taken a liking to the son of a family who lived on a farm that adjoined Rockwood and had paid for his education, as his parents could not afford to do so. The boy, Charles C. Whitman, had prospered by working as a gilder and had moved to New Orleans. Harry bumped into him and was greeted with great affection and expressions of gratitude to his father. It was an opportunity for Whitman to repay his debt to the Tudors, and he loaned Harry five hundred dollars to cover the shortfall on the cost of freight for the icehouse and the purchase of a site. Frederic inevitably drew a moral from this tale when it was told to him by Harry in a letter home: "It shews what industry is capable of effecting & how wasteful is luxurious indulgence in which all our family were educated."

Harry not only found a site and got the icehouse put up, he had the initiative to buy a cargo of ice from a ship that arrived from Marblehead, the port just to the north of Boston, ahead of Frederic's first consignment. Frederic waited anxiously for news from Harry, who appeared to be doing a good job at last. On July 12, 1821, he got a letter that almost bowled him over: sales were running at four times what he had hoped for, bringing in forty dollars a day. Elsewhere, his ice trade had collapsed or was in trouble. The business in the West Indies was gone, at a huge loss, and the trade in Havana had suffered further disasters. First an icehouse manager had been killed in a robbery, then his successor had died. Without New Orleans, the market Frederic had been close to abandoning a few months earlier, he would have been ruined. Like a man who has been saved from falling over the edge of a cliff, Frederic promptly collapsed. The signs had been there in January 1821, when he wrote in his diary:

> Last night in a state of hallucination I asked of God his kindness. I solicited some relief from this continuation of excessive anxieties which harass your very soul. Exert yourself a little longer, cherish hope, and spare no cost of care or time or thought, and victory shall be yours.

He had fallen ill in April after catching a cold, had recovered a little, and then had developed a fever that confined him to his bed. In bold letters in his diary, he printed "ANXIETY" in capitals on several different days. He was unable to do anything, and lay in bed all day. That autumn there was no member of the Tudor family in Boston to care for him, but his brother-in-law Robert Gardiner was called for from Maine. Gardiner was a friend of Frederic's physician, a Dr. Jackson, who said his patient was very ill and needed someone to stay with him.

A nurse was attending Frederic, and Gardiner worked with her in shifts so that the patient was never left alone for more than a brief period of time. Dr. Jackson had prescribed the regular rubbing of Frederic's body, and Gardiner took his turn. By early in the new year, Frederic was beginning to show signs of recovery, and his sister Emma, Robert's wife, came to Boston to see him. Dr. Jackson insisted that the only cure for Frederic was freedom from all care and anxiety; he recognized the fact that his patient had suffered a mental breakdown. Emma suggested he take a convalescent trip somewhere in the south. When Frederic protested that he could not, for his ice business would collapse, Robert offered to take over until his return. It is some measure of Frederic's desperate condition that he agreed to this, though Robert recalled him saying in his "droll manner," "What a fool you must be to make yourself my drudge, and allow me to go off to take my ease and recreation."

Robert Gardiner not only handled the financial side of Frederic's business in Boston, he topped up the reserves with his own money whenever they were running low. It was an act of charity for which he appears to have been given little credit, for he recalled that he never asked for or was offered any interest on the money he put into Frederic's ice business. However, Frederic did write to his mother, "I can not say what would have become of me but for his stepping in to relieve me at this time."

Frederic did not, of course, simply take a vacation. Instead, he sailed to Havana in late January to see how the business was faring. He had appointed a new icehouse keeper, John Damon, formerly in charge in St. Pierre. Frederic's ship *Bearing* was well armed with blunderbusses and guns in case of attack by pirates, who were causing concern to West Indian shipping—only two years earlier his cousin William Savage had been badly treated and robbed of his watch and ring. The *Bearing* got through without incident, and Frederic was back in Havana on March 1, 1822. He intended only to make sure the ice business was running smoothly again, then to sail on to New Orleans to meet up with Harry so they could take a trip up the Mississippi and back to Boston overland. However, he stayed a whole year in Cuba, and then went straight back to Boston, where he found his business in impeccable order under the management of Robert Gardiner. His established markets were now—in addition to Havana—Savannah, Charleston, and, best of all, New Orleans. The trade was increasing and he was having to build new ice-houses in all these cities. He was now nearly forty years old, and was in a mood to capitalize a little on his success.

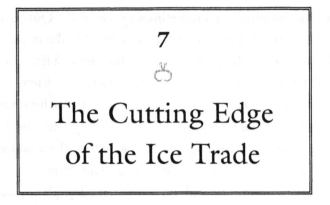

7

The Cutting Edge of the Ice Trade

When Frederic returned to Boston from Havana in 1823, he had recovered his health and was making enough from his established markets to feel relatively secure. His brother Harry had succeeded in promoting ice sales in New Orleans beyond Frederic's wildest expectations, and this became the mainstay of the business. In Frederic's absence, Robert Gardiner had paid off most of the debts and had kept the books in good order.

Frederic began to take long walks, which he felt were good for his health, to relax, and to think of new projects. For the time being, the ice business could carry on without making too many demands on him. One of his favorite excursions was to Nahant, an island in Massachusetts Bay twelve miles north of Boston. A thin strip of land joined Nahant to the coast, but this was covered at high tide and it was most easily reached by a short boat ride. For a number of years, it had been a place for

Bostonians to picnic, and sometimes to stay, as the Quaker families who farmed it as pasture for cattle would take in boarders in the summer. In 1823, the first steamboat service from Boston to Nahant began, and a hotel was built there by a friend of the Tudors, Thomas H. Perkins. Very rapidly, it was becoming a fashionable summer resort for wealthy Bostonians, and Frederic's mother, Delia, put together what money she could glean from the family to have a small cottage built there. Very soon, Frederic took this over and turned her modest plans into the foundation of a small country estate. Rockwood had been sold, and Nahant was to be its successor, with Frederic very much the lord of the manor.

Building of the Nahant cottage began in 1824, and the following spring Frederic hired a farmworker to help him create a kitchen garden, which included some two-year-old asparagus roots that would sprout that year. He sometimes sailed his boat the *Ohio* across the bay to carry provisions to Nahant; at other times, he took the steamer or walked or rode along the narrow strip of land that connected the island to the coast at low tide. While the new building was being put up, Frederic rented a cottage on Nahant, and the family began to gather there in the summer of 1825.

Frederic was now forty-one years old and, as far as the ice trade was concerned, resting on his laurels. He was not going to be rich, but he could expect to be comfortably off. He had no family of his own, and the Nahant estate gave him a great deal of pleasure, as he loved planting things and watching them grow. Another project had occurred to him, too. Salt was still an expensive commodity, and he wondered if the seawater that surrounded Nahant could provide him with extra income. In a small way, he began a saltworks in which seawater was evaporated in heated pans. He also wondered if the power of the tides might be harnessed somehow.

While Frederic was otherwise engaged in 1825, one of his ice suppliers had been working on a technical improvement that was to completely transform the industry. He was Nathaniel Wyeth, whose father owned a hotel on the shores of another fashionable Boston resort, Fresh Pond, in the countryside outside Cambridge (the use of the word "pond," as in Walden Pond or Spy Pond, is misleading, for anywhere else most of these "ponds" would be regarded as lakes). Fresh Pond has a shoreline that runs for about two miles; it might take ten minutes to row across in a leisurely fashion, taking the longest line from shore to shore. The *American Magazine* for December 1835 described it as "a beautiful lake, or sheet of water . . . which has long been a favorite resort for the inhabitants of Cambridge and Boston and the students in the University . . . It is little more than a mile distant from the Colleges and on the north side of a public road leading from Boston into open country."

It was a playground for Harvard students, who went boating and fishing in summer and skating in winter. The Fresh Pond Hotel was well placed to cater to other visitors from Boston as well as those from the colleges, and was a convenient resting place for farmers on their way to market. The hotel, like the farms on the shores of the lake, had its own icehouse, which was filled each winter from the pond. Nathaniel Wyeth was born there on January 29, 1802, and spent his childhood and youth helping to run the hotel and exploring the countryside around it. His father and elder brother had both been educated at Harvard, but, like Frederic Tudor, Nathaniel had no taste for academic life. When he was twenty-two, he married his cousin Elizabeth Jarvis Stone and continued to live at the hotel, earning his keep by helping to run it. He would have joined in the ice cutting from the time he was a boy, and by the 1820s, he was one of Frederic's suppliers.

Although the hotel was popular, it did not provide Nathaniel with the kind of income that would enable him to offer his new bride, a member of a prosperous family, the comforts she might expect. Selling ice gave him some extra money, but the amount he could make was limited because harvesting ice was such a slow and backbreaking business. Everything was done by hand, with large blocks broken away with pickaxes and chisels, then cut into manageable pieces on the shore with large-toothed, two-man saws like those used for cutting timber planks from tree trunks. Alternatively, a hole would be hacked in the ice to allow the saws room to work, and blocks would be cut out, then hauled ashore, floating on the free water beneath.

The demand for ice generated by Frederic Tudor's trade set Nathaniel Wyeth thinking about more efficient ways of cutting it. By 1825, he had arrived at the idea of harnessing a horse to a metal blade that would cut into the ice as it was dragged over the surface of Fresh Pond. Wyeth left no diary or account of how he arrived at this mechanism, and we can only assume he was inspired by watching the skaters on the pond in winter and the horses plowing the fields in summer. The only really detailed description of his invention is in the official record of his application to patent it a few years later. An issue then was whether or not his ice-harvesting contraption was fundamentally different from a carpenter's plow—a plane with an adjustable blade that cut grooves and moldings in wood. If the force needed to push it was too great for the carpenter, a rope would be tied to the front of the "plow plane" and his apprentice would add extra power by pulling it along while the carpenter steered it.

Wyeth would have been familiar with this tool, and it may have helped give him the idea for his ice plow, which could be pulled by men but was more effectively hauled by a team of two horses. The horses would be shod with spikes, as they were when in winter they hauled sleighs, snowplows, or wagons along the icy New England roads. By 1825, steam engines were driving all kinds of machinery, but they were heavy and cumbersome, and not suitable for ice cutting. There were not yet any gasoline-powered engines; throughout the nineteenth century horses provided the motive power that drove all road vehicles, hauled farm machinery, and distributed the goods that ships and railways brought into towns. Though the century is often characterized by the excitement and novelty of the railroad, horses were vital for the growth of industries and cities. The horse-drawn ice plow may look to us now like some kind of throwback to an earlier era, but it was not an anachronism in the nineteenth century. In remote regions of America, it was still used until the early 1950s.

Wyeth improved on his first models until he had a plow that, as it cut a first groove, would scratch a parallel line into the surface of the ice. So the first run marked the line for the second, and so on, until an area of the frozen surface of Fresh Pond was neatly marked out. He then turned the horses so they would draw the plow back across the already marked surface at right angles. When this was done, the pattern of the ice blocks was drawn, and he could begin to cut farther into the ice until the grooves were deep enough for the cubes or rectangles to be prized out with iron chisels. Wyeth's new ice plow had great advantages over the existing methods of harvesting. Cutting was much speedier, and larger quantities could be harvested in favorable weather. It was a form of mass production that effectively reduced the cost of ice. As the large plowed ice cubes were much more even than those cut by hand, they could therefore be stacked more efficiently in icehouses and ships' holds, which also meant that they melted more slowly than irregular chunks of ice.

Frederic was greatly impressed with Wyeth, considering him, as he wrote to Harry, "just enough of a schemer and inventor to be valuable." He paid tribute to him in his diaries, remarking that he was "of singular excellence" and "active and intelligent." Wyeth was also a young man after Frederic's own heart, eschewing the academic world for a practical and profitable life in business. In November 1826, Frederic offered him five hundred dollars a year to take charge of cutting, storing, and loading his ice supplies for the coming season, and was very pleased when he accepted. Frederic had shown that ice could be stored, shipped, and sold a long way from where it formed. Wyeth demonstrated that it could be mined, or harvested, in huge quantities.

After a long hearing, Wyeth won his case that his invention—a brilliant adaptation of two existing rural tools, the horse-drawn farmer's plow and the carpenter's plow plane— was, essentially, new, and he was granted a patent in 1829. But, just like other tools used in the countryside, any blacksmith could forge an ice plow, and it was not easy for him to profit from his invention.

Wyeth's basic harvesting implement, along with some other innovations he devised for the hoisting of cut ice from the pond to the icehouse, would within twenty years or so transform America into the first refrigerated society, and make New England a major exporter of ice to countries as far away as India. All the scientific and technological endeavor that went into finding a way of manufacturing ice artificially failed to render Wyeth's ice plow obsolete. While this may appear surprising, there is a simple explanation. The science of heat, or thermodynamics, was not properly understood until the very end of the nineteenth century, and it was inhibited by an age-old misconception about hot and cold. A big question was: "Where does cold come from?" and there was debate about whether it was from air, water, or the earth. In fact, natural ice is the product of great environmental forces. The sun provides the power, heating the earth. That heat dissipates through the atmosphere. Natural greenhouse gases, first identified in the mid-nineteenth century, trap some of the heat irradiating from the earth's surface and maintain a temperature high enough to support life on earth. Without these gases, the earth would be frozen solid, because the balance of heat gain from the sun and heat loss from the earth would be such that its temperature would be below zero. For artificial refrigeration to work, a way had to be found to create conditions in which one object or substance was so cold that when it was brought into contact with air or water that was above freezing, the temperature balance would be low enough to form ice. To achieve this requires energy, and the corollary of artificial cold is artificial heat. For example, domestic refrigerators give out heat and raise the temperature in a kitchen at the same time as their interior temperature falls.

It was theoretically possible in the 1820s to make ice with steam-powered machinery that drove pumps to create a vacuum in which gases such as ether fell to very low temperatures, but this was expensive. The most effective source of power for creating the conditions for artificial cold was electricity, but this was not widely available in America and Europe until well into the twentieth century. For refrigerators to be efficient, they required a pumping mechanism and a technically complex system of recycling the refrigerant used. The synthetic replication of the interplay between the sun and the earth, which creates the Arctic and Antarctic regions and brings winter and ice to large regions of the Northern and Southern hemispheres, was no simple matter.

In the 1820s, there was no question of artificial refrigeration competing with the natural-ice trade; the only force that might inhibit that trade's development was the fickle New England winter. A minor drawback of Wyeth's ice plow was that the ice had to be thick enough to support the weight of the horses and the men driving them. A mild winter could therefore present greater problems than it would have in the days of hand cutting. But the first winter of the new Tudor-Wyeth ice business, in 1826–27, went well. As the next season approached, Frederic prepared for a bumper crop, and sent his brother Harry off to Charleston and Augusta, Georgia, to put up new icehouses. Harry went on to Savannah, where, for lack of time, he rented an existing store and fitted it out with insulation. All the while, Frederic wrote him letters offering, in turn, both encouragement and rebuke. He praised Harry's success in New Orleans, but was infuriated by an incident in which an icehouse keeper had gotten drunk and bragged about the level of sales. "It is absolutely necessary that I should be *obeyed*," Frederic wrote in February 1827. "I *must* be a dictator." He signed the letter "yrs affectionately. F."

Frederic had nothing but admiration for young Nathaniel Wyeth, who as the winter of 1827–28 set in was already working on a new system for raising ice blocks into the icehouses on the shores of Fresh Pond. When the ice had been broken with chisels into separate chunks, it was coaxed along free-water channels to the icehouse entrance by men holding grappling hooks. Hauling these chunks out of the water and stacking them was heavy work, and Wyeth wanted to speed it up. What he devised was rather like a weighing machine. Two wooden platforms were hung on ropes from either end of a tilting beam, so that when one platform was in the water, the other was up in the air. The lower platform would take on a block of ice, and by means of a pulley system a horse would haul it up, at the same time lowering the other platform, which would then be loaded with ice while the first was being unloaded through the top hatch of the icehouse. In his diary, Frederic produced a little sketch of it.

At first the winter of 1827–28 began promisingly, with cold snaps in November and good freezing weather in early December, each day's thermometer reading being recorded by Frederic in his diary. But then the daily temperatures began to rise and fall in a worrying manner. One day it would be freezing or below, the next in the fifties. There was some ice, and Wyeth harvested it for the hotel and for local buyers, especially butchers and dairymen, who were using it more and more. This was an indication of the spread of the use of ice on a commercial scale throughout America. In 1828, the *New England Farmer* would reproduce in full Thomas Moore's pamphlet on the design of icehouses and refrigerators, originally published in Maryland in 1803.

Ice six inches thick would do for local use, but Frederic needed thicker blocks, which would last better, for export. The time to start harvesting with the new horse-drawn plow seemed to have arrived on Christmas Eve, with a hard frost and Fresh Pond covered in rapidly thickening ice. It had reached eight inches when the temperature rose above freezing again, and the ice was spoiled by rain. Wyeth cut no ice for Frederic in December, and by the middle of January, with continued warm days, things were beginning to look desperate. Ships had been booked to take the ice south, and if their cargoes arrived late, Frederic would have to pay compensation. In his anxiety, he went almost every day to Fresh Pond, often walking from his lodgings in Boston, more than four miles away. His diary entry for January 13 reads:

> Thermo 45 . . . I found Wyeth wandering about the woods at Fresh Pond in all the lonely perturbation of invention and contrivance. His mind evidently occupied in

improving the several contrivances which he is perfecting for carrying into effect improvements in his several machines for the Ice business . . . For minds highly excited and in great activity there is no Sunday.

At last the weather hardened, and Frederic wrote: "The frost covers the windows, the wheels creek, the boys run, winter rules & $50,000 worth of ice now floats for me upon Fresh Pond." Two weeks later, his profit was melting away again, and he began to discuss with Wyeth how they might solve the problem. He noted on January 27:

> Thermo 32 wind east, overcast. Got into a horse and chaise and went to Wyeth's to consult with him in the present emergency what should be done. The pond is so thawed on the edges as to be absolutely inaccessible for wagons. All the roads are heaving with mud. But I found Wyeth had already debated and determined and was at work with 8 or 10 men. Wyeth is equal to a difficulty which to common minds seems insurmountable. He was on the pond without hat or coat. He had forgot that the Thermo was at the freezing point. In his yet unsettled plans he found warmth of circulation, from the calm-seeming, but, in fact, vigorous action of his mind.

Wyeth cut ice whenever he could, finding areas that had been shaded in the day, and often working with his men at night. Frederic began to spend time at the Charlestown wharf, reassuring the shipowners that supplies were on their way. To make the best of what ice there was on Fresh Pond, Wyeth adapted his hoist so that blocks were shot straight into waiting wagons that squelched off slowly along the thawing muddy roads. By the end of January, Frederic was writing to Robert Gardiner, now back in Maine, where the winters were harder than in Massachusetts, asking him to gather some emergency stocks from the Kennebec River, which always froze solid.

The harvesting on Fresh Pond went on into the middle of February, with Wyeth working every day and night to gather what he could before the ice was gone and the weather too mild for any more to form. Orders were coming not only from the established markets in the south, but from New York and Boston itself, and the cost of ice was rising. It was a first intimation of the ice "famines" that were to trouble New York and other big cities later in the century whenever they experienced what was known as an "open winter" and the Hudson River and the lakes did not freeze over.

Wyeth had not been the only person cutting ice on Fresh Pond: several rivals owned sections of the shore and had started local ice businesses. One of these, a man named Stedman, offered to sell Frederic his ice. After a good deal of haggling, he bought it and loaded it straight onto a ship sailing south.

Wyeth himself abandoned Fresh Pond, and went in search of smaller stretches of water that might have remained frozen because they were shaded from the sunshine by trees. He found one not far away, in the district of Malden, only five miles from the wharves in Charlestown, and started cutting at once. Frederic promised bonuses to Wyeth and the teamsters driving the wagons if they could get a good quantity out to fill his ships, which were waiting to sail. He also wrote to Robert Gardiner asking him to cut more ice, as he now believed the summer demand would drive prices to very high levels.

What should have been a demonstration of the ingenious new techniques developed by Wyeth began to turn into a farce as the desperate search for ice continued. The isolated stretch of water Wyeth had found was called Swain's Pond, and he and Frederic were excited by the fact that no one except a few small-scale local harvesters knew it held a treasure trove of thick ice. However, when Wyeth and his men turned up at midnight to begin cutting, they discovered that in the narrow lane leading to the pond was a large rock that would prevent their wagons getting in and out. The local farmers had no idea that their pond was about to be stripped of its frozen water until they were awakened by a violent blast. Wyeth had removed the rock with gunpowder. In the morning, the farmers and their families saw wagon trains lumbering up the lane, loaded with ice, and that was the scene Frederic found when he arrived to inspect the work. He could not drive his carriage down the lane because of the wagons, so he took down a fence to get into a farmer's orchard. When he was reproached for this act of vandalism, he offered to pay for the fence to be mended. A farmer told him he had been awakened in the night by the blast and had taken in some of Wyeth's men who had been injured by a flying piece of shattered rock. Frederic gave him twenty-five cents.

The owner of the land then appeared, and Frederic quickly negotiated a deal whereby for ten dollars he could clear some of the shoreline of bushes and trees so that ice could be stacked there while awaiting the wagons, which were making very slow progress along the rutted, muddy roads. Wyeth then made a deal with another man who had come to harvest ice at Swain's Pond, whereby Wyeth would cut it for him for $2.50. All the ice on Swain's Pond therefore cost Frederic and Wyeth only $7.50, but the expense of getting it out kept rising. The teamsters, or wagoners, constantly increased their fees, and Frederic incurred further expense when temperatures rose into the sixties and rain began to dissolve the ice and he had three hundred yards of sailcloth sent from Boston to hang from some remaining trees in an effort to shade the last ice from the midday sun. When one of the horses fell into the pond and had to be rescued, and the wagoners complained that the roads were impassable, the little ice mine was abandoned. Frederic and Wyeth went in search of other local ponds, but what ice they found was not worth cutting.

Toward the end of February, Frederic asked Wyeth if he would be willing to "change his latitude" in search of ice—in other words, to head up to Maine, where there was plenty on the Kennebec River. As always, Frederic made this a cloak-and-dagger exploit, telling Wyeth to creep out of town in the early morning of February 26. As soon as Wyeth and his men had gone, the temperature at Fresh Pond dropped to way below freezing. Some of the men who had stayed behind began to cut ice locally, while Frederic put in orders from harvesters in Bath, Maine. There was no shortage of workmen in winter, for the farms were mostly idle, and in Cambridge there were men available from the brickworks that closed down for the season.

Frederic relished these frantic weeks, his enthusiasm rising as the price at which he could sell his hard-won ice rose to record levels in the southern markets. He did have more rivals in the trade now, but he had the best team and the best methods, and he would make good profits. By March 1828, Wyeth and Gardiner had stacked an enormous quantity of ice on the banks of the Kennebec, where it was preserved in temperatures that still hovered around freezing. Wyeth sailed to New York, Philadelphia, and Baltimore to sell ice, while Frederic began to relax back in Boston, knowing he now had all the supplies he needed. By May, he was back at Nahant, tending his garden and working on his country estate. It was then he heard that a large part of the Kennebec ice had been washed away by a freshet, a surge of freshwater brought on by the spring thaw. That calamity cut his profits for the year, but he and Wyeth still did well.

In 1828, Frederic took stock in his diary of the way in which the ice trade had grown. He was still far and away the leader in the Boston trade, which was now shipping around four thousand tons annually, compared with twelve hundred tons in 1816. The biggest market was New Orleans; then came Havana, Charleston, and Savannah. He had many rivals now who simply copied his methods of cutting, storing, and shipping ice. There is little or no information on who these competitors were or how they fared, for the ice industry was not regulated or documented in any way until much later in the century, and only Frederic has left detailed accounts of the business. It seems fair to assume, however, that harvesting ice had become a regular winter trade that gave work to farmhands and others whose industries had to stop in hard weather. Cutting ice was casual work, paid by the hour or the day.

When Frederic gleefully jotted down in his diary that fifty thousand dollars floated for him on Fresh Pond, he was taking a very optimistic view of the profits to be made. The loss of ice between harvesting and its eventual sale was always huge: Wyeth estimated some years later that only about one-tenth of the ice cut was eventually sold. Insulation never stopped the ice from melting—it simply slowed down the rate of loss when the temperature was above freezing. Onboard ship, stowed ice would melt at the rate of several tons a day, and the crew had to constantly pump water from the bottom of the hold, not because it would sink the ship but to help preserve the ice.

As long as there was enough ice left to sell at a reasonable rate, profits could be made, but they could not be calculated on the number of tons cut or shipped out of Boston. In a mild winter like that of 1827–28, the price of ice in the market would rise, but so too would the cost of harvesting it. To persuade the wagoners to go on working in dreadful conditions, Frederic had to continuously offer bonuses and higher rates of pay. He could never be sure what the balance of these expenses and the income from sales would be.

The frantic measures that had been necessary to gather ice at the very outset of their partnership must have had an influence on Wyeth and Frederic's view of the future prospects of the industry. Though it gave Wyeth a living and provided Frederic with reasonable profits, it was still, as the *Boston Gazette* had put it in 1806, a "slippery speculation." Frederic was always on the lookout for new ventures, and in 1828, he and a partner reopened an old black-lead mine on 127 acres of land at Sturbridge, in Massachusetts. Black lead, or graphite, was the raw

material for the manufacture of crucibles used in smelting met-
als, and there appeared to be a ready market for these. Frederic
opened a small factory in Boston and began production in
November. There were teething troubles as always, one of
which was the flooding of the mine. Frederic called Wyeth in to
help, and he soon solved the problem with a windmill that
pumped the water out. As the mining of the lead could only be
carried out in the summer months, this was a useful supplement
to the ice trade for both of them. Now, in addition to the ice
trade, Frederic had his estate at Nahant, his saltworks, and his
black-lead business.

Wyeth too was making a reasonable living, not only working for Frederic but building up a business of his own supplying
Boston with ice, as well as managing the Fresh Pond Hotel. But
the circumstances of the two men were very different. Although
he was the younger of the two by nearly twenty years, Wyeth
was married, while Frederic was still a bachelor, now forty-
seven years old and living in a boardinghouse in Boston.
According to notes in Frederic's diaries, Wyeth's young wife
had a drinking problem, which gave her husband an incentive
to get away from Fresh Pond.

In 1828, a young widow from Philadelphia named Elizabeth Keating had visited Boston and caught Frederic's eye. The
two of them had danced joyfully at the Nahant Hotel, and had
spent time together before she returned home. Frederic then
visited her, and asked her to marry him, but in the end she
turned him down on the grounds that she did not want to live
in an unfamiliar town. The affair had continued through 1830,

and when it was over, Frederic asked that all the letters he had written to Mrs. Keating be returned.

Besides his wife's drinking, the inspiration for Nathaniel Wyeth's escape from Fresh Pond, where he had spent all his life up to the age of twenty-nine, came with the propaganda of a charismatic figure named Hall J. Kelley, who urged the young people of Boston to better themselves by education and adventure. After the triumph of the Lewis and Clark expedition, the first to cross America from east to west in 1814, Kelley joined in the clamor to persuade adventurous Americans to settle the Oregon Territory, which was not then claimed by the British or any other foreign power. In 1831, Wyeth joined the society Kelley formed to encourage the settlement of Oregon and began to plan his own expedition, but then realized that Kelley himself was not going to practice the virtues of the pioneering that he preached. In letters to family and friends, Wyeth made it clear that he was not going to Oregon with any patriotic motives: his interest was solely in establishing trade links that he believed would make his fortune.

Naturally enough, Frederic did not want to lose his right-hand man, and tried to persuade Wyeth to stay. On January 6, 1832, he noted in his diary: "Wyeth announces to me his determination to leave my employ in consequence of his domestic inquietude. It is a great loss to me." When he realized that he could not dissuade him, Frederic helped to fund the expedition, which included twenty-three men Wyeth had gotten together, all making some contribution to the cost. The idea was straightforward: they would cross America by boat and wagon train until they reached the Columbia River, where they would set up a trading post to deal in furs and Pacific salmon, which would be salted and sent back to Boston and other eastern cities. Provisions for the trading post would be dispatched by ship around Cape Horn, to meet the overland expedition when it arrived. Most of Wyeth's capital for the venture came from his family and friends, but when he was still short and anxious to leave, Frederic guaranteed a loan of $2,500 in return for Wyeth's ice plow patent.

Wyeth and his men sailed from Boston on March 11, 1832, leaving Fresh Pond and the ice business to Frederic, who reassured his most trusted employee that if things did not work out in Oregon, he could always come back. The ice plow and other innovations Wyeth had made in the loading and storing of ice had put the business on a new and potentially much more profitable footing, greatly reducing the cost of the annual harvest in those years when winter did not "rot in the sky." Without knowing it, Wyeth was leaving just at the point when the frozen-water trade was about to enter a new and exciting era made possible by his own inventiveness. Frederic did not know that either.

In fact, in 1831, when Wyeth had Oregon on his mind, Frederic was also preoccupied with an adventure that he believed might soon eclipse the ice trade, and without any physical effort at all. There would be no wading through mud or dragging wagons down rutted winter roads, no anxiety about the weather or haggling with shipowners. His cousin William Savage, who had been his first Havana agent in the ice trade, persuaded Frederic that the way to make real money without effort was to speculate not in the growing demand for cold drinks, but in the craze in America for hot coffee. At the time, about eighty million pounds of coffee was consumed in the United States each year, and the country's population was rising at the rate of 750,000 annually. Europeans were also drinking huge amounts of coffee. Frederic was hooked by Savage's brilliant idea that all you had to do was promise to buy bags of coffee at the going rate, wait for the price to rise, then sell it at a profit. There was no capital outlay needed, just a guarantee that you could pay no matter what happened—in other words, offer a surety, which in Frederic's case was his ice business. When Frederic first began to speculate, coffee prices were rising at 20 to 30 percent a year, so he kept on buying. By the time Wyeth was on his way to Oregon, Frederic had put $250,000 into coffee and was still buying, calculating his future profits in terms of millions of dollars.

All the assets of the ice business were in hock to coffee, and in May 1832, as he arranged for a consignment to be sent to New Orleans, Frederic noted in his diary: "I believe this is the last cargo of ice I shall ever ship." He handed over much of the running of the ice trade to a young man named Francis Richards while he enjoyed his market garden at Nahant, took long walks along the coastline, and went fishing in a new, catamaran-style boat he had designed. Early in 1833, he noted that he had committed himself to buying between five and six million pounds of coffee—about 15 percent of the annual consumption in America, and enough to provide a million Americans with all they needed for a year.

Wyeth, meanwhile, was fighting pitched battles with Black-feet Indians on his way to Oregon. He wrote to Frederic occasionally, hoping his coffee venture was going well but urging him not to abandon the ice trade, which was now a solid business that Wyeth himself might take up again if his own speculation in fur and salted salmon failed.

8

A Cool Cargo
for Calcutta

In the spring of 1833, Frederic was a familiar figure in
Boston—not quite the "Ice King" he would become, but a
respected merchant who had made his contribution to the
prosperity of the town in a trade nobody but he had regarded as
feasible a few years earlier. He lived in a boardinghouse, as single gentlemen did at the time, and spent many enjoyable days
out at Nahant tending his asparagus and other vegetables. About
town, he always wore a blue frock coat, and his small frame—
even at the age of forty-nine he weighed only about 137
pounds—cut a dashing figure on State Street when he mingled
with other merchants. But the coffee speculation worried him,
as he was aware that if it went wrong, he could lose millions of
dollars and his entire ice business, which gave him what prosperity he had. Neither the salt nor the black-lead ventures were
going to return significant profits.

The ice trade was now an established business in Boston, and harvesting with copies of Wyeth's ice plow a routine winter activity in Massachusetts. Frederic was not the only ice shipper, but he was recognized as the authority on the techniques of the trade. In April, another Boston merchant, Samuel Austin, approached him and asked if he would be interested in an exciting joint venture. Boston had a regular trade with India, but on the outward journey ships often went loaded only with ballast. Austin was not in the ice trade himself, but believed that if Frederic could pull off the spectacular feat of sending cargoes of ice to the chief Indian ports of Bombay, Madras, and Calcutta, it would, in general, stimulate shipping to the East Indies.

Frederic was immediately enthusiastic. He noted in his diary that for years he had wanted to send ice to India but had not had the capital to risk it. Now it had fallen into his lap. Within a week, he had engaged a brig, the *Tuscany*, to carry the ice, and had agreed with Austin and another partner, William Rogers, that they would each have a third interest in the enterprise. They would make Calcutta, then headquarters of the British East India Company, their first port of call. Frederic's old enthusiasm for the ice trade was rekindled. He supervised the fitting out of the *Tuscany* himself, noting in his diary on May 4:

> Over to Charlestown twice today. The Calcutta ship will be nearly completed in the fitting tonight. The space alloted [sic] for the ice will admit about 60 cords [a cord is a measure of volume rather than weight, but sixty cords of ice was equivalent to roughly 180 tons] to be put on board—fitted first with a sheathing of boards one inch from the skin of the vessel—then 6 inches tan on the bottom—

6 inches hay stuffed and rammed in on the sides. Then one foot boards of lumber on the bottom—then a foot deep of tan on the sides and the bulk heads one foot thick of dry tan rammed in hard—boarded under the beams and a foot of tan or perhaps 20 inches all dry and connecting with the tan of the bulk heads and side so as to make an unbroken stratum on top ends sides and bottom. Weather very dry and dusty.

Despite the care he took to insulate the ice, Frederic was not entirely confident of the success of the experiment. On May 7, he wrote:

Dry, warm, dusty. Twice over to Charlestown today to look after the finishing of the loading of the ship Tuscany which is now complete. She has 60 cords on board and fitted in a most thorough and expensive manner and if she does not carry her cargo safely to Calcutta and arrive with ⅔rds of it no ship ever will and the undertaking should be abandoned.

Frederic was impressed with the unique and historic nature of this voyage. He wrote to Captain Littlefield, who was commanding the *Tuscany*:

As soon as you have arrived in latitude 12° north you will have carried ice as far south as it has ever been carried before, and your Ship becomes a discovery ship and as such I feel confident you will do everything for the eventual success of the undertaking; as being in charge of the first ship that has ever carried ice to the East Indies.

The *Tuscany* finally sailed on May 12, with William Rogers as supercargo, or agent, onboard. It would be his job to take care of sales in Calcutta. Frederic calculated that the sixty cords of ice would melt at a rate of around fifty pounds an hour over the four-month voyage, and that 120 tons should remain when the ship docked at Calcutta.

Sadly, there is no record at all of how the *Tuscany* fared on the high seas with its historic cargo of ice. Captain Littlefield left no journal or any account of the voyage, and no logbook has been found. However, it is possible to gain some idea of what the voyage must have been like from accounts written later. The captain and crew would have been under strict instructions not to open the hatches, and to keep the ice sealed in and protected from seawater, which would dissolve it very rapidly. Even when the *Tuscany* approached the stifling seas of the equator, the crew could not touch the ice in the hold. Their only contact with it was the task of continuously pumping out the meltwater, which was added to the routine shipboard work of scrubbing and sail mending, and was not regarded as onerous. The crews of the East Indiamen from Boston were an elite, chosen from local boys who had first gone to sea at the age of about thirteen and who learned their trade from captains who were often only in their twenties. They were well provisioned with fresh food in these days before there was any refrigeration at sea.

In the 1840s, Captain Charles Barry, a homesick Boston sailor, regularly wrote to his wife, Sarah, while aboard the ship *Delhi*, which carried ice to India for Frederic Tudor. His letters give a vivid description of his routine at sea:

> As this is Sunday, I think I should write down how I have spent the day. A little after six this morning, I went on

deck and had a good bath with a couple of buckets of sea water, and a good scrub with a sponge and two coarse towels. After that, I walked a while on deck, then took breakfast. After that I read several chapters in the Bible, then whiled away the forenoon as best I could. Dinner came—a plate of pea soup, a side bone of goose and cranberry sauce, pickles and so forth. Potatoes don't grow here, so we did without them. We closed off with plum pudding made without milk or eggs. We are 113 days out today, but, as you perceive, we are not entirely without fresh food. We have three pigs, four geese and a dozen chickens still left.

There were many opportunities to catch fish. Captain Barry sent his wife an amusing account of some deep-sea angling in the Indian Ocean they enjoyed on a sultry April day:

Yesterday we saw three sharks. The shark hook was baited and hung over the stern. It was not long before one of the gentlemen was safely hooked under his jaw with a stout hook attached to a piece of chain. He was hauled on the deck. The men took the shark to the gangway, cut him open and what do you suppose was found inside? The feathers of a chicken. About four hours before, when our decks were washed, a chicken was thrown overboard and this was the lucky shark that found that delicious morsel. I mentioned this to show what powers of digestion sharks must have. In not more than four hours, not a bone, not a leg or the least vestige of the chicken was found in him but the feathers.

In his memoirs *Old Sailing Ship Days* (1908), John Whidden, a Marblehead sea captain who as a young sailor went on two trips taking Tudor ice from Boston to India, recalled that fresh fish were often caught, and that some ships were loaded up with livestock, like Noah's ark. Whidden tells the story of the unfortunate consequences on the *Brutus* of Captain Meacom's attempt to tidy up the ship by getting the carpenter to construct a model house for the animals onboard, to replace all the pens that cluttered the ship's deck. The model animal house was ingeniously compact:

> On each side were very large coops that drew out and pushed in like a chest of drawers. On one side were kept the geese, the other ducks, and the other two chickens and fowls. In the centre were the goats, while the whole upper part was devoted to pigeons, who roosted on the joists, and flew around the ship, passing back and forth through the holes made for them, always returning at night to their coop. By the time we were up with the Cape, the cook had made large inroads upon them, but there still remained a goodly number, besides the pigs that were kept in the large sties forward by themselves.

As if to confound Captain Meacom's desire for neatness aboard the *Brutus*, a huge rogue wave hit the ship in the Indian Ocean. Young Whidden saw it coming and saved himself from being washed overboard by wrapping a rope around his body and tethering himself to a spar:

> The next instant the crash came. Driving with the force and fury of an avalanche the wave swept over us, starting the forward house, filling the decks with water and knocking the model stockhouse into smithereens, while the livestock were in a moment swimming and floating around the deck.

All the crew were safe, and they grabbed as much of the half-drowned livestock as they could. Whidden had a pet onboard, a dog named Dash that in rough weather usually curled up in his master's cabin or stateroom. The sliding door to this room had been left open when the wave hit, but had slid shut when the ship righted itself:

> On opening it when I went below, after all was in order again, to change my wet clothes, a comical sight met my eyes. My pillow was occupied by a big goat, who glared defiance at the dog, who stood at the foot of the berth, and a pig reclined in the center, while all around were chickens, geese, and pigeons wringing wet, and everything in the room, bedding and bedclothes were soaking.

Apparently the cargo remained firmly in the hold of the ship—it was only the decks and living quarters that were wrecked by the wave.

Among the pets commonly kept onboard were monkeys of various kinds, which were expert climbers of the rigging and a great amusement for the sailors. But certain species were apt to steal the livestock. Whidden recalls an occasion when three "Sumatra monkeys"—perhaps orangutans, as he describes them as standing three to four feet high and being a dirty yellow color—stole a chicken cooked for the captain's dinner. Despite the valiant attempts of the sailors to retrieve the fowl, they could not match the monkeys' agility. In a rage, the captain and officers got out their pistols and, ignoring the protests of the crew, who were fond of their pets, brought the monkeys down with a fusillade of bullets.

The *Tuscany* would certainly have carried livestock, the crew would have fished in the southern seas for bonito and shark if they saw them, and over the four months of the voyage they would have lived the all-absorbing life aboard the square-riggers of those days. For days on end, they would not see another sail, but when they did pass a ship, a kind of semaphore was used to pass messages that might provide rough-and-ready information for those waiting back home. Otherwise, news of the fate of the crew and its cargo would arrive by letter long after they had reached their destination. Frederic Tudor would not hear of the outcome of this historic voyage until early in the following year. In the meantime, while the *Tuscany* was crossing the equator for the first time en route to the Cape of Good Hope, Frederic became totally absorbed in a new and far more momentous project. He had fallen in love.

Frederic's rooms were in Pearl Street, at the time a fashionable part of Boston. For a long while, he lived in a boardinghouse at number 3, run by a Miss Betsey Leakin, but when he had prospered he took the house next door, had a door cut between the two buildings, and lived in relative seclusion while still eating at Miss Leakin's table. There were sometimes distinguished visitors staying at the boardinghouse, who livened up the dinner conversation. One who stayed for several months was the great American painter of birds John Audubon, who impressed Frederic with his dedication to his work—he allowed himself only a ten-minute break for meals. In February 1833, Audubon bought a live golden eagle from the Boston Museum, and brought it back to the boardinghouse to study it for the second edition of his classic *Birds of America*. In order to pose the eagle in the way he wanted, it was necessary to kill it. He tried to do this by asphyxiating it with burning charcoal, but when that did not work, he stabbed it to death. Clearly this was no run-of-the-mill boardinghouse. In June, after Audubon had painted and disposed of the eagle, a young woman and her aging aunt came for a short stay.

When Frederic, now nearly fifty years old, with white hair and weathered face, saw Euphemia Fenno at Miss Leakin's dining table for the first time, he was smitten. Euphemia, or Effie as she was known, was thirty years younger than he, just nineteen, and turned many heads in Boston as well as Frederic's. On one occasion, Effie and her aunt were invited to dinner at the Nahant Hotel along with Frederic and others. Clearly, her aunt was keen for her to find a suitor, and regarded Frederic as a reasonable prospect, despite his age. He courted Effie, attending balls and dinners and inviting her and her aunt out to his Nahant cottage to eat dinner by the sea. Effie referred to him as her "old bachelor."

Effie had an impressive pedigree. Her great-grandfather was the Earl of Pemberton, who in 1770 had been granted twenty thousand acres by King George III in what was to become New York. Effie herself was not wealthy—her father kept a modest store in an out-of-the-way place in New York State called Mount Upton. But Frederic was not looking for an heiress: he was lonely, and madly in love. His diary contains some truly uncharacteristic entries toward the end of July 1833, including: "Love Loving—Kiss Kissing and then the lover, sighing like a furnace made to his mistresses eyebrow"—disjointedly quoting Shakespeare's *As You Like It*.

Inevitably, the course of Frederic's love did not run true. Effie soon returned to Mount Upton, followed by a constant stream of love letters from Frederic. In September, he took a trip with his brother Harry to New York State to look over some salt-works and enjoy a break from business. As he was going to be near Mount Upton, he wrote to Effie to ask if he could visit her. By the time he was ready to turn back to Boston, he had heard nothing, and assumed that he had been rejected. Nobly he wrote to her:

> . . . thus ends the beautiful dream of an old bachelor . . . Let us place your short visit to Boston in July 33, as being a point of felicity in our lives which is to be valued, because all happiness is necessarily short, in this passing scene, in which it is absolutely dangerous to be joyful.

Prepared once again for disappointment, Frederic was startled to receive a letter from Effie when he was on the stagecoach back to Boston. She did want to see him. Though it was too late for him to turn back, he was soon to return to Mount Upton. On Sunday, October 20, he proposed to her, and four days later she accepted. Frederic went back to Boston anxious to keep his engagement a secret. He wrote to Effie explaining that he had fallen out with his mother and his sister, although he still supported them financially, and that she and he might suffer ridicule because of the difference in their ages:

> I . . . do not wish to be joked upon taking to wife a girl (as will be said) of fourteen. If we have made up our minds to do this thing, it is our own affair, and it will be far better to accomplish it first and let the world add their own comments and notes of admiration afterwards, than to have heartless impertinence talking over what is no business of theirs and about which they really care nothing.

To Frederic's annoyance, news of his engagement was leaked to a Boston newspaper, but he planned to keep his native city's prying eyes away from his young bride by getting married in New York State. The wedding day was fixed for January 5, the following year, 1834.

While Frederic was falling in love in July 1833, Nathaniel Wyeth, the man who had revolutionized the harvesting and storing of ice without which the Calcutta venture would not have been possible, was on his way back from Oregon after an appalling catalog of misfortunes. All his party of twenty-three men were gone. Some had deserted him early on, several had died of disease, and some had been brutally slaughtered by Indians who resented his expedition's intrusion onto their land. The British Hudson's Bay Company had taken him in, and probably saved his life. They were his rivals in the fur trade, and though they treated him well, they made it clear that they would oppose any attempt he made to set up in competition.

Wyeth had to fight his way back to Boston with a new band of men he had met up with in Oregon. A diary entry for July 1833 gives his description of the end of one of them:

Thompson, having been out hunting and fatigued from loss of sleep, was dozing. He was awakened by a noise among the horses, and, opening his eyes, the first thing that presented itself to his sight was the muzzle of a gun in the hands of an Indian. It was immediately discharged, and so near his head that the front piece of his cap alone saved his eyes from being put out by the powder. The ball entered the head outside the eye, and breaking through the

cheek-bone, lodged in the neck. While insensible an arrow
was shot into him from the top of the shoulder downwards.

Wyeth also wrote letters. It was not easy to post them, and a few,
like the following one to Frederic, were marked "Not Sent."
However, they give an idea of his state of mind at the time:

> If I am unsuccessful this is my last effort and however
> disagreeable it may be I shall then return home, and solicit
> again the place which your generosity once honoured me
> with . . . In some of your last communications to me you
> hinted your intention of quitting the ice business. I hope
> you have not done so. It is a good permanent income to stand
> upon in case of disastrous speculations to which all are
> liable. I anticipate that you have realised much money from
> your coffee operations. I can not see how you can fail of
> making some. Be assured if my wishes would avail anything
> you would make plenty. I am now writing in the open air. I
> am shivering with cold, badly clothed in skins. Here there is
> no wood to warm one and all nature seems clothed in gloom.

In September, Wyeth killed an elk, noting: "Very acceptable as
we had had nothing to eat since yesterday noon; saved his horns
for my best friend Mr F. Tudor of Boston."

On November 8, he was back in Boston, where Frederic
greeted him heartily and said he hoped Wyeth would now get
back to the business of harvesting ice. He offered him a greatly
increased salary and urged him to abandon what he called his
"wild goose chase." But Wyeth had not given up on Oregon,
and was already planning a new scheme: to send ships around
Cape Horn carrying supplies he could sell to the Pacific fur

traders in the mountains, and to make up return cargoes with salted salmon. To raise funds, he gave talks at which he put on display two Indians he had brought back, one Flathead and one Nez Percé. He stayed in Boston long enough to look after the ice business while Frederic went off to Mount Upton to get married. So neither Wyeth, still intent on making his fortune on the other side of the continent, nor Frederic, in the thrall of his romance, were as concerned as they might otherwise have been about the fate of the *Tuscany*.

All the interest, all the excitement as the ship with its historic cargo approached the Ganges delta in September 1833 was with the British community in Calcutta. They had been told to expect a consignment of New England ice, but many had doubted that this was anything more than some kind of practical joke. The *Calcutta Courier* reported on September 6 that it had news that the *Tuscany* had already "arrived in the river," and that it was in fact loaded with ice:

> The Yankees are so inventive, and so fond of a joke at the expense of the old country, that we had some misgivings about the reality of brother Jonathan's frozen manifest, and suspected him to be coolly indicting a hoax upon the wonder-loving daughters of Britain. But the circumstantiality of this announcement stimulated our enquiries, and we are thereby enabled to add a few particulars to the article which we copy from our contemporary.

The "contemporary" was the *India Gazette*, which had broken the news of the *Tuscany*'s arrival. It too had thought the idea of importing American ice was "hopeless," but had been encouraged to learn that "one of the gentlemen engaged in the present venture has for many years supplied the southern section of the United States, the West India Islands and several ports in South America."

The British community anticipating the arrival of the ice had a tantalizing wait as the *Tuscany* made slow progress up the Hooghly River. Calcutta, founded in the seventeenth century as a fort and trading post by the British East India Company, lies about seventy miles inland from the Indian Ocean. It could take days or even weeks for ships to navigate the treacherous Hooghly, with an East India Company pilot aboard with his retinue of servants. The *Tuscany* would pass Saugar Island, notorious for its tigers, whose roars would curdle the blood of ships' crews at night, and steering clear of shoals and sandbanks edge its way against the strong current of the river, toward the Calcutta docks.

The temperature at the mouth of the Hooghly was around ninety degrees Fahrenheit when the *Tuscany* took on her river pilot on September 5, 1833. The ship's progress and the state of its cargo became the subject of intense interest and some excitement in the Calcutta newspapers. The first concern was for the survival of the ice. The *India Gazette* reported that only a third of the cargo had melted, and that Calcutta might soon enjoy what some other countries regarded as

> if not a necessary, at least a common luxury of life—its use not being confined to the table, but extending to medical practice, as an auxiliary, and in some cases even as a primary cure in many of the fevers and other acute diseases peculiar to the tropics.

The *Courier* received two conflicting reports. One was from the supercargo, Mr. Rogers, who said that only 10 percent of the ice had been lost. The other had it that the *Tuscany* was now drawing only thirteen feet, whereas it had drawn fourteen when it reached the mouth of the Hooghly, suggesting that a good deal more ice had melted. The paper complained that the ship should have had one of the new steamships to tow it upriver so that more of the ice could be saved, for "since the vessel entered the river the pumps have indicated an increased ratio of daily wastage by the increased heat of the surrounding water and atmosphere." The *India Gazette* argued that the ice should be declared free of duty before it reached the wharves at Calcutta, so that it could be unloaded right away, and that the normal prohibition on discharging cargoes at night should be lifted, to allow the ice to come ashore in the cool of the evening. So eager were the British authorities for Boston ice that both concessions were granted before the *Tuscany* reached Calcutta.

Triumphantly, the *India Gazette* reported:

We are happy to state that the Board of Customs, Salt and Opium have authorised the landing of the cargo of Ice . . . free of duty and have directed that every facility may be afforded in the Customs' Department for its conveyance, without delay or impediment, from the ship to the godown or place of store. An extra tide-waiter, at the charge of the importers, is to be placed on board the ship to see that nothing else be discharged from it into the boats destined to land the Ice; and that officer is to be instructed to allow the Ice to be removed from the vessel at night, should the importers consider that as the most favourable time for landing it. The tan and other articles used in the packing as non-conductors of heat, are either to be destroyed, or, if landed, to be subject to the usual duty leviable on such articles . . . The attempt to import this article does credit to the enterprise and its success to the skill, of American bretheren [sic]; and although they doubtless contemplate their own advantage, it is equally certain that all those to whom they may render this luxury accessible, by its abundance and cheapness, will participate in the benefit.

Back in Boston, Frederic could not know of the triumph of the *Tuscany* as it docked in Calcutta with its ice duty-free and in instant demand. It was September 13, more than a week after the ship took on its Hooghly River pilot, before the unloading of the ice began. The *Courier* reported, beginning with an allusion to the misguided scientists of *Gulliver's Travels*:

This Ice importation beats the old scheme of extracting sunbeams from cucumbers . . . We have submitted our vaporising selves to the condensing influence of the *Tuscany*'s Ice-Bergs, which we had this morning the gratification to see landing briskly from the vessel. These blocks are beautifully transparent and of great size, some of them nearly a foot thick (Boston winters must be very severe). Coolies were carrying them across the Strand in the sun— the large pieces without any covering—to deposit them in the small godown in a pucka building at Brightman's Ghaut, which has been floored with wood for the purpose.

Though the true figure was never established, Frederic claimed that the *Tuscany* lost a third of its cargo in the course of the voyage, which would mean it had well over a hundred tons to unload in Calcutta. The unloading, which continued into the daytime to the surprise of the *Courier*, was quite a spectacle. William Rogers, who was in charge of the operation, told them that he thought it better to get all the ice off the ship as quickly as possible. It was a lengthy operation, which John Whidden described some years later in his *Old Sailing Ship Days*:

> Along the water front of the city are great mooring buoys, where the ships lie in tiers of twos and threes. The landings opposite these tiers, running up the bank from the river's edge, are called 'ghauts'. Going into moorings in the inner tier to discharge our ice, a bridge of boats was made, with a plank walk about four feet wide, from the bank to the ship, ice blocks being hoisted from the hold and lowered over the ship's side upon the heads of three coolies stationed to receive them. It was very hot, and the moment the cold water began to trickle down their black backs, they would shiver, and strike a beeline for the ice-house, never stopping until their load was off their heads.

On Saturday, September 14, the *India Gazette* paid a visit to the ice ship: "We went on board the *Tuscany* last night to inspect the mode in which it has been stowed; and found the poor fellows engaged below in landing it, although well clad, shaking with cold from head to foot as if with the ague." The following day, the *Courier* took a look in the makeshift icehouse: "We stood before the mass in store, which we were told was already about fifty tons, and felt the same delightful sensation from the refreshing radiation which we once experienced in a hot day in February on entering the Caves of Carlee."

On September 17, the *Courier* carried an advertisement:

ICE AT BRIGHTMAN'S GHAUT, STRAND

The ice brought by the *Tuscany* from America will be for sale every day, from Monday next, after sun-rise, at Brightman's Ghaut, Strand in quantities of not less than one bazar [sic] seer, at the rate of four annas per seer. Purchasers should send a woollen-wrapper or a basket of rice-chaff, either of which will preserve a few seers for twenty four hours. No saltpetre or salt should be placed near the ice.

The inhabitants of Calcutta are invited to sustain this undertaking. The present cargo is not expected to last longer than sixty days, and no further supply will arrive until next June, nor then unless the present shall meet with a ready sale.

W. C. Rogers

Frederic's ice was a sensation in Calcutta. The British community felt that if the trade could be continued, it would have a profoundly beneficial effect on their daily lives, and was determined to do everything it could to encourage regular deliveries. A committee was soon formed to collect subscriptions to build an icehouse—not a wooden American structure, but a grand stone edifice more fitting to the "city of palaces," as Calcutta was known. In fact, the proposal for an icehouse was being discussed in the *Calcutta Courier* even before the *Tuscany*'s cargo was landed. The reporter had heard of the icehouse in Havana, and looked forward to the time when Calcutta would have ice "on such a scale of price and supply, as shall not only render Ice creams a common and constant luxury of the table, but likewise afford a cheap and more efficient substitute for Saltpetre, for cooling liqueurs."

The British in Calcutta were quite obsessed with keeping cool, and until the arrival of American ice they had made do with what was available locally. A preparation of saltpeter (which was abundant in Bengal) and water made a cooling mixture in which to immerse wine and beer for the table, and there was also very expensive local ice made by an ingenious method that had been used for centuries and was, in a sense, an early form of artificial refrigeration. During the winter season north of Calcutta, cool winds would blow and the temperature at night might fall to the low forties Fahrenheit, or even to near freezing. To make ice, shallow pits were dug and filled with straw. Onto this were placed porous earthenware containers, and into these were poured a few inches of previously boiled water. As the cool winds blew around the pots, the process of evaporation froze their surfaces, producing a thin film of ice. Before the heat of the day could melt this, it would be gathered and stored in pits, from which it was sold in the hot summer months. It was an expensive process: on the reckoning of one observer, two thousand laborers working on a huge acreage of land might collect twenty-five to thirty tons of ice in a night. The ice brought by the *Tuscany* was of quite magical quality compared to the locally manufactured alternative, which was sometimes referred to disparagingly as "Hooghly slush."

For the British community in Calcutta, the Americans who had sent the ice, about whom they knew practically nothing, were worthy of the highest honor. The *Calcutta Courier* put it this way:

> The first transport of Ice, from the shores of the United States to the banks of the Ganges, is an event of no mean

importance; and the names of those who planned and have successfully carried through the adventure at their own cost, deserve to be handed down to posterity with the names of other benefactors of mankind—the importer of the potato into Europe, the disseminator of useful plants in regions where they were unknown, and the authors of every species of discovery.

However, as Frederic Tudor was involved in the enterprise, establishing a regular ice trade with Calcutta was not a straightforward matter, and very nearly ended in farce. On January 31, 1834, Frederic received the news that the *Tuscany* had arrived safely in Calcutta. He wanted to send three more cargoes of ice right away, but his partner Samuel Austin would not agree to his terms, and the two "authors of discovery" had a falling out. William Rogers stayed on in Calcutta, and it was he who was on hand to enjoy the tributes of the British, though he had never before had anything to do with shipping ice and was soon to disappear under mysterious circumstances. While Frederic and Samuel Austin were having their falling out, Rogers was presented with a silver-gilt cup by the highest British authority in Bengal. It is inscribed:

> Presented by Lord William Bentinck, Governor-General and Commander-in-Chief, India to Mr Rogers of Boston in Acknowledgement of the Spirit and enterprise which projected and successfully executed the first attempt to import a cargo of American ice into Calcutta—Nov 22nd 1833.

Frederic first heard about the presentation to Rogers in March, noting in his diary that the cup was a "silver vase in commemoration of the event of the introduction of Ice from the United States to Hindoostan." But he never saw it, or its full inscription, which does not mention him at all.

Rogers did not return to Boston, but set up in Calcutta as a boardinghouse keeper. It was said that he also practiced as a part-time dentist. This gave rise locally to a story that the first importation of ice to India was the work of an American doctor who was presented with a silver cup that he then sold to set himself up in business. It is possible that Rogers claimed some medical expertise, and that he did sell the cup, but there is no conclusive record of what happened to him. The Calcutta newspapers make some reference to his involvement in attempts to get together a subscription for the building of an icehouse, which came to nothing. Lord Bentinck's silver cup disappeared, and was presumed lost somewhere in Calcutta. Then, in the 1980s, a retired social worker, Anne Halliday, brought it to the Heritage Plantation Museum in Sandwich, Massachusetts, to ask what the strange inscription referred to. It had been found among her father's collection of seafaring artifacts when he died in 1928. Her brother had taken it, and for fifty years kept it as a curiosity on his farm in Tennessee. It then came back to Miss Halliday, who was living on Cape Cod, and she became interested in the inscription. She was finally directed to the Peabody Museum in Salem, Massachusetts, which has a small exhibit on the ice trade, but they were as puzzled as she was: they knew of Frederic Tudor, but had never heard of Rogers. They finally pieced the story together from Frederic's diaries.

First Rogers was awarded the cup that Frederic thought was rightfully his, then Samuel Austin sent a cargo of ice to

Calcutta on his own. On April 22, 1834, Frederic noted in his diary:

> Mr. Austin is loading the Tuscany with ice for Calcutta thus endeavoring to steal away from me this business: but he has engaged Stedman who has run himself and everybody he has had to do with ashore and the Tuscany may be considered as having done better than she will do. I am taking measures.

Stedman was the ice harvester who had sold a cargo to Frederic in the dreadful winter of 1827–28.

It looked to Frederic now as if the glory of the Calcutta trade was slipping away from him, and he had a mind to pull out of it altogether, even though in May he learned that each of the three partners—himself, Austin, and Rogers—had made a profit of $3,300 on the *Tuscany*'s pioneer shipment. The ice had lasted until December 1833, and had sold well. While Austin's cargo was headed for Calcutta, Frederic sent ice to Rio de Janeiro in June, and he heard in October that it had made a reasonable profit of over a thousand dollars. But he was worried about the costs of opening up a regular trade with Brazil.

Toward the end of 1834, Frederic began to realize that his coffee speculation was headed for disaster, though he did not yet know if it would ruin him. He decided to make one last effort to wrest the Calcutta trade from Austin and the others who were now sending speculative cargoes to India. As always, he was determined to demonstrate that he was the Ice King, and that interlopers would be driven out. In December, he began to fit out the *Apthorp* to take ice to Calcutta, and had decided that he would send with it a long letter to Lord Bentinck in which he would point out that the only reason the *Tuscany*'s shipment had been successful was because of his own involvement. It began:

> It is with much satisfaction that I have observed the notice which has been taken by your Lordship and the Indian Public of the enterprise planned by me, nearly twenty-nine years ago: but which a variety of circumstances, adverse to its accomplishment, have prevented my carrying into the full effect which I have now realized in the shipment of a cargo of Ice in the Tuscany, Captain Littlefield . . . last year.

Frederic continues with a paragraph on his Martinique venture, to establish his precedence in the ice trade, then goes on:

> Anyone who undertakes an enterprise of this kind has not only its incidental dangers to encounter, but the jeers, opposition, scorn of mankind at its commencement, and the robbing of its advantages when success has given its sanction. I have experienced the first, and my undertaking has for a long course of years been vexed with attempts to crop the fields which I have cleared, and to reap the harvest where I have sewn the seed. These attempts heretofore have been attended with universal disaster, and the fear that they will continue to result in the same way, is the cause of my now addressing you this note.

The letter continues with an account of the falling out with Austin, who Frederic says is bound to fail. Frederic had already received the gratifying news that the second voyage of the *Tuscany* had not been very successful, as the ice had been poorly loaded and the ship limped into the Indian Ocean listing badly. As for himself, Frederic had considered turning his back on the whole affair:

> Were I to consult my ease and my comfort, I should perhaps allow this Indian enterprise to fail; to pass away, as a thing to which chance once gave a small success; but which after experience and further trial proved to be at first indebted to accident alone: but I feel that I am bound to give it success, and not allow the enterprise to fail, however sorely harassed it may be by persons such as I have spoken of above.

Frederic points out that William Rogers, who had now disappeared, knows nothing of the ice business, and hopes he did not give the people of Calcutta the impression that he was some kind of expert. He wants it publicly known that he has fallen out with Rogers and Austin, and that he would like to continue in the trade himself: "to conduct it, as I originally planned it, and India may have a delicious and high luxury, at a price little above the lowest necessaries of life." In fact, he states finally, he would like ice in India to become a "common and cheap gratification." To that end, he is sending out an agent who does know the business, and introduces the Governor-General to his new representative in Calcutta, Marcus Bacon, an odd-job man from his Nahant estate.

Along with the letter, Bacon was given a thirty-page instruction manual on how to conduct the ice trade. He would have plenty to organize, for Frederic had decided that buried in the *Apthorp*'s 150 tons of ice would be 359 barrels of Baldwin apples, the same variety he was now sending to Havana and his markets in the southern states, some boxes of grapes, some walnuts, packs of butter, and a large quantity of cheese. He put samples of all of these into one of his own icehouses to see how well they would keep.

On December 19, 1834, Frederic saw the *Apthorp* weigh anchor and head out of Boston Bay, carrying with it his credentials as the most successful and knowledgeable shipper of ice in America, indeed the world. The cornucopia of Massachusetts luxuries was due to reach Calcutta around the middle of March 1835. If it was successful, and Lord Bentinck accepted Frederic's case for being Calcutta's sole provider, he was sure he would make good profits from adding India to his ice empire.

At about the same time as the *Apthorp* left Boston, Frederic's cousin William Savage, who had been the instigator of the great coffee speculation, went bankrupt, owing two hundred thousand dollars. Frederic confided to his diary his own desperate financial position. He had bought and sold about seven million pounds of coffee and still had half a million pounds to sell at a loss he calculated would be $175,000. This figure later had to be adjusted to around $210,000. On the other hand, his ice business was going well, as the demand for his cargoes in Havana, Charleston, and New Orleans was rising. He reckoned from this and other small investments that he had made about a forty-thousand-dollar profit for the year.

His marriage had clearly given him a new lease on life, for he wrote: "I do hope reward, and do expect much future happiness, and I expect it more because I am happy at this time in despite of the great loss of property which the year has exhibited." He had lost, he said, four times the amount his wealthy grandfather had been worth. But he anticipated that his ice business in the next six years would give him an annual income greater than this same ancestor's entire worth.

The confidence he expressed in these terrible circumstances must have struck those close to him as near madness. He owed almost a quarter of a million dollars, and his creditors would not release him from his obligations. They suggested that he carry on his ice business as their agent, and that they would have the power to restrict his personal expenses to a sum they decided on. Frederic refused, arguing that they would do better to leave him to get on with the ice trade himself and pay them back, with interest.

His creditors agreed to give him his liberty, and he could now add to the profitable business with Cuba and the southern states the potentially lucrative Calcutta trade. He noted that the failure of the coffee speculation, which had ruined others, had been "attended with some good effects in my case." It had invigorated him and made him determined to pursue the Calcutta trade, which "had nearly been abandoned by me from laziness."

There was no news of the *Apthorp* until August. It had not yet reached Calcutta but was still at sea, having suffered serious damage to its wheel while rounding the Cape of Good Hope. On October 1, having had no further word of the fate of the ship and its cargo, Frederic opened the samples of apples, grapes, walnuts, butter, and cheese he had kept in his icehouse at Fresh Pond and found that they were mostly in good condition. They had been stored for nine months, so there was still a chance that the *Apthorp*'s cargo would be intact even after a very long voyage. Still confident, Frederic sent a fresh consignment of 162 tons of ice and two hundred barrels of Baldwin apples to Calcutta on the *Concord*.

A few days later, a letter arrived from Marcus Bacon that told the sorry story of the *Apthorp*. It had reached Calcutta after a voyage of 163 days, and had only two tons of ice left when it docked in the first week in June. All the fruit and dairy produce was ruined. Starved of ice, the British made a scramble for the remaining two tons. The *Bengal Hurkaru* reported on June 6:

> Although proceeding from the Captain's own mouth, it turned out to be a false report that the *Apthorp*'s Ice had melted away. For the last two days there has been a delivery of Ice to all applicants on board the vessel at the very moderate price of two annas per seer, and we observe Messrs Gunter and Hooper are now advertising Ice Creams, as if we were in the month of February or March instead of June. This is the first instance in which Ice has been offered for sale in Calcutta (if Dr Wyse's Hooghly experiment two years ago be not an exception) under a perpendicular sun; but we fear the luxury will be of very few days duration.

In the same issue, Frederic's letter to Lord Bentinck was printed in full: Marcus Bacon had delivered it right away, and it had presumably been passed on to the *Hurkaru* as a document of general interest. The newspaper, clearly unaware that the letter had been carried on the ill-fated *Apthorp*, wondered why it had taken so long to arrive, as it was dated December 1834. However, its comment on Frederic's manifesto was favorable:

From this communication we collect that we are likely to have rival speculators in the field. There is nothing like competition; but we may be forgiven as Mr Tudor was the originator of a plan for supplying hot climates with Ice, for wishing him that greater success which his knowledge of the business matured by long experience seems likely indeed to insure for him.

Just as Frederic wished, his letter prompted the British citizens of Calcutta to gather in the town hall and debate the pros and cons of giving him a monopoly and raising a subscription to build a proper icehouse. After much heated discussion this is what they did. Gratified by this display of confidence in his abilities, and as the man who should have received Lord Bentinck's silver cup, Frederic was inspired to present a trophy of his own to the captain of the *Apthorp*. It was a silver cup burnished with gold inside and inscribed:

A token for Geo W. Stetern who commanded the Bg *Apthorp* in a voyage from Boston to Calcutta in India in the year 1835 when that vessel had cargo of Ice part of which was preserved and sold after having been on board from December to June. In remembrance of this remarkable fact, this cup is presented by the owner of the cargo I am T [Tudor] 1836.

9

The Ice Wagon
Rolls On

The only way Frederic could pay off his $210,000 in debts from the disastrous coffee speculation was with his profits from the ice trade. He felt confident he could do so, because he was now making about forty thousand a year from the business, and it was still growing. There was the new market in Calcutta, but more significant was the steady rise in the consumption of ice in America. When the New Orleans trade had begun in 1821, one shipment a year would satisfy demand; now Frederic was sending cargoes throughout the summer. It was the same with Charleston, Savannah, and the inland towns of South Carolina and Georgia that had ice shipped to them along the rivers.

Frederic's main source of ice continued to be Fresh Pond, the shoreline of which was now transformed by his timber icehouses and those of his rivals in the trade. Though he held the patent on Wyeth's ice plow, Frederic appears to have done nothing to enforce it, so there would be several teams out on Fresh Pond when the ice was ready. Nobody witnessing the scene could have failed to be impressed by the scale of the industry.

A Boston physician, Benjamin Waterhouse, who had known Fresh Pond since boyhood, was amazed at the changes he found when he returned to live in Cambridge as an old man. Waterhouse was a controversial figure who had championed the use of vaccination against smallpox in the early 1800s and had spent many years in the West Indies. On his eighty-second birthday on March 5, 1836, he noted in his diary:

> The snow thick and thick solid ice still remains, and cubes of ice from Fresh Pond incessantly, from before daylight to after sunset, pass in six-horse teams without an interval of half an hour. Numerous and huge wooden buildings are run up in Charlestown ready to be shipped off for the Southern States, even to Louisiana, the Bay of Mexico, the West India Islands and the East Indies! The quantity shipped is incredible, as there is as yet no tax upon it, the profit immense, compared with our laborious brickmakers. Besides this, which passes in front of my house, there are three other avenues to Boston through which this luxury is passing in quantities absolutely incredible . . . the cubes being 12 to 18 inches square incur but little diminution in the Dog-days.

Close to Fresh Pond were long-established brickworks that closed down in hard weather, and the ice trade provided the brickmakers with temporary work in the winter. As more and more ice was harvested, Fresh Pond attracted migrant laborers who stayed in boardinghouses during the winter. In January

1837, Frederic counted 127 men, 105 horses, and 1 bull employed in the Fresh Pond business, including 60 men just supplying him with ice. A smaller permanent workforce was needed throughout the year to look after the icehouses and to load up the wagons when an order came in for a cargo. Boston itself now used several thousand tons of ice a year as the domestic icebox became popular and butchers, fishmongers, and dairymen were able to rely on a supply of ice throughout the summer to keep their produce fresh. In fact, all the cities along the eastern seaboard were rapidly developing Tudor-style ice harvesting and storing techniques, and were cutting ice locally using Wyeth's ice plow, which was easy to copy and could be made by blacksmiths wherever it was needed. By the late 1830s, horse-drawn wagons appeared in the streets of New York delivering "Rockland Lake Ice," which was regarded as of the best quality, coming from a crystal-clear stretch of water in the hills to the north of the city.

In 1805, when Frederic and his first partner in the business, his elder brother William, had first dreamed up the idea of selling Rockwood ice to "tropical climates," there was no market for it anywhere in America, and they never imagined that there would be. Now, thirty years later, the trade they had pioneered had given rise to the technology that made the regular supply of ice to Americans possible throughout the summer. An entirely new industry had been established with the harvesting and sale of a commodity that had previously been regarded as valueless. William, whose scheme to fund the New Orleans venture in 1820 had been vital, did not live to witness this triumph. He had continued with his literary career for a few years and then, still short of money, had gone to South America to seek his fortune. He died there on March 1, 1830.

On February 13, 1836, Frederic wrote in his diary:

> This day I sailed from Boston thirty years ago in the Brig Favorite Capt Pearson for Martinique: with the first cargo of ice. Last year I shipped upwards of 30 cargoes of Ice and as much as 40 more were shipped by other persons . . . The business is established. It cannot be given up now and does not depend upon a single life. Mankind will have the blessing for ever whether I die soon or live long.

At this time, Nathaniel Wyeth was still on the Pacific Coast, struggling desperately to establish his business of shipping out provisions for the fur traders and bringing back salted salmon. When he had left Boston in February 1834, he had planned to be away for just a year. He had crossed the continent on riverboats and with wagon trains in time to meet the ship he had sent around Cape Horn loaded with equipment he would sell to the fur traders in Oregon. The expedition and the arrival of his ship had been timed to coincide with the run of Pacific salmon that would be salted down and would make up the return cargo. But, like Frederic's *Apthorp*, Wyeth's ship did not come in on time. When it was halfway up the west coast of South America, it was hit by lightning and had to put in to the port of Valparaiso, Chile, for repairs. When the ship finally did reach Oregon, it was too late for the salmon. Wyeth dug in for another year, building a small wooden outpost he called Fort Hall in what was to become the state of Idaho. He never entirely lost touch with Frederic, and wrote on October 6, 1834:

I find by some English publications that your ice adventure to the East Indies attracts much attention . . . I am
anxious to hear how the speculation ended and if you find
sufficient encouragement to continue it, also how your
ordinary ice business has succeeded the last year and what
has been the result of your coffee affair.

On the same day, he wrote to Effie's relative James Fenno, who
was then looking after Frederic's finances in the ice trade:

I think of the old business and hope if this fails to find
an opening left to resume it. When I shall be at home is
uncertain. This business looks very bad at this time. We
have failed in everything for the first year. I shall do all I
can one year more.

By September 1835, Wyeth had to concede that his salted
salmon venture was a failure. He wrote home:

Dear Wife, I have been very sick, but have got well, and
shall be on my way to the mountains to winter at Fort Hall,
in about six days. I expect to be home about the first of
November 1836 . . . I have sent you a half-barrel of
salmon, which I hope will be in good order. I cannot attend
to putting them up myself, therefore they may not be so
good. The season has been very sickly. We have lost by
drowning, disease and warfare seventeen persons up to this
date and fourteen now sick.

Frederic had lost everything with his speculation on coffee, and
Wyeth had now failed completely with fur and salmon. The ice
trade was to be his salvation too. When, sick and tired, Wyeth

got back to Boston in October 1836, Frederic went to see him right away to talk about reemploying him. He wined and dined him in Boston, giving the adventurer who had often gone days without food a lunch of broiled chicken, steak, and partridge at the Rice Tavern. The two sparred a while over terms, but Wyeth had no alternative but to work for Frederic again, and Frederic was very anxious to have his most successful and loyal associate in the ice trade back in the business. A deal was worked out that, in effect, gave Wyeth three times his former salary.

That first winter after his return to Boston, Wyeth had found Fresh Pond crowded with rivals. There had been a rough-and-ready agreement that anyone who owned some of the shoreline could cut ice on that part of the pond that abutted their property. At first this had not presented any real problems, because there was more ice in a good winter than could ever be harvested—in his diaries, Frederic mentions several winters when the pond froze again after the first harvest, so a second, and sometimes even a third crop could be gathered. However, in 1840, one of the farmers who owned a section of shoreline put up an icehouse so large that it suggested he was intending to cut much more than his fair share of ice. If this continued, there was likely to be a serious conflict: disputes over the rightful ownership of ice became quite common and violent later in the century, when the trade was at its peak. Though he worked for Frederic, and had a cut of Frederic's profits, Wyeth also owned his own section of shoreline, and had his own business cutting and selling ice. To maintain the peace on Fresh Pond, he suggested that all the harvesters agree to call in an arbiter.

In keeping with New England's tradition of solving problems at town meetings, the harvesters agreed to set up a commission headed by a Harvard Law School professor, Simon Greenleaf. The principle Professor Greenleaf arrived at was that each harvester's share of the winter ice should be based on the length of shoreline he owned, regardless of the total size of the property that abutted the pond. A surveyor was commissioned to make a very detailed map of Fresh Pond and its frontage, on a scale of two hundred feet to the inch. Lines were drawn on it to define the boundaries of ownership in the form of an irregular spiderweb, for the circumference of the pond is not a neat circle.

This beautifully produced colored map was first published in September 1841. It shows that Frederic, with just over forty-eight acres of Fresh Pond, and Wyeth, with nearly forty-four acres, were far and away the largest owners. When the ice was a foot or so thick, about a thousand tons could be cut from one acre, so in a good winter, their holdings represented a potential crop of more than forty thousand tons each from Fresh Pond alone. There were seven other owners, all with less than 10 acres, the smallest share going to a Mr. Richardson, who had a mere 2.72 acres.

When the harvesting began, the owners could easily mark out with stakes their own patch on the ice. Now that the ice trade was so valuable, this method of establishing ownership was essential, and it became widely used elsewhere as the industry grew. A special problem arose on rivers, for a sudden thaw could wash substantial areas of ice downstream, removing it from the ownership of one proprietor and delivering it to another. There would be anguished cries of "Hey! That was my ice!" and disputes would arise, as they sometimes did later in the century on the Kennebec River in Maine, where a rush of freshwater brought on by mild temperatures could dislodge even very thick ice and send it crashing toward the sea.

While the ownership of the Fresh Pond ice was being determined, Wyeth—who had received an unexpected amount of money, having managed to sell Fort Hall to the Hudson's Bay Company—was involved with a number of other businessmen in a project to promote a railway that would carry the ice from Fresh Pond and the smaller Spy Pond nearby, which provided a reserve supply when needed, to the ice sheds at Charlestown Harbor. Frederic had no part in this: he appears to have been happy with the trade as it was, and content to leave it to others to invest in this modernization. It was not that he was uninterested in mechanization: in fact, he could claim to be the first person to bring a steam engine to Boston, a small half-horse-powered machine that he had shipped up from Charleston in 1830. He wrote at the time:

> Steam will soon take the place of horses in ordinary stage coaches and I should not be surprised if it should be employed for heavy draft and ordinary purposes. The times are surcharged with novel inventions and improvements of all kinds. Steam seems now the ordinary power: in all probability some other and more convenient one will be discovered.

Though there were experiments with steam trains in the 1820s, the building of America's railways did not get going until the 1830s. The importation of British locomotives, which were designed to run on well-laid tracks without great inclines or sharp curves, was a failure on the American tracks, which were put down at great speed and were notoriously dangerous. Lighter American locomotives, with a swiveling four-wheeled bogie at the front, solved some of the problems, and short stretches of track were built in many places. Boston had a line built in 1837 to link its granite quarries to the wharves at Charlestown. This ran out toward Fresh Pond, but terminated four miles short of it. Wyeth and his associates wanted it extended, and published in 1840 what they called a "Brief Statement of Facts" in justification. The authors of this manifesto made liberal use of capital letters to drive home the significance of ice as a New England resource, a reality that Boston apparently still found difficult to come to terms with. The "Brief Statement of Facts," as well as giving a vivid account of the ice trade at the time, bristles with indignation that the trade is not taken seriously enough. The final paragraph reads:

> *ITS OPPONENTS* concede that if Massachusetts had a *COAL MINE*, it would be entitled to a *RAIL ROAD*. This is virtually the coal mine of Massachusetts and if *ENGLAND* has enriched herself by Rail Roads to develop her *COAL MINES* and *MASSACHUSETTS* has gained wealth by giving a Rail Road to her *GRANITE QUARRIES* why should not she gain equal advantage by a *RAIL ROAD* to her *ICE MINE*, which rivals coal and granite in its importance to the shipping interest, and contributes as much to the refreshment at the *SOUTH* as coal does to the comfort of the *NORTH*.

A railroad, the promoters argued, would reduce the overall cost of harvesting ice by a third by greatly reducing the wastage between the time it was cut and stored and its delivery to Charlestown. They gave a very high figure for the overall loss due to wastage before the ice went on sale in "the tropics": 90 percent. This meant that only a hundred tons out of every thousand cut was actually sold—or, as they put it, "charge upon ten tons must finally be borne by one." Much of this wastage took place during the cumbersome hauling of the ice by track and road to Boston Harbor. The forty thousand tons annually harvested for export and home consumption was taken in heavy wagons that carried five tons each, and their weight cut deep ruts in the mud.

> The ice when carted, as at present, is greatly injured by jolting over rough roads in consequence of which the corners of the squares are broken off, much ice wasted, and close stowage (which is essential to the preservation of ice in a long passage) prevented.

Often the wagons could not negotiate the roads at all, and ships waiting for their cargoes were held up—charging the harvesters for the delay.

These factors, said the promoters of the railroad, were holding back a new local industry that had invested fifty thousand dollars in large icehouses on the shores of Fresh Pond and Spy Pond, in addition to the costs of cutting, shaping, storing, and moving the ice ("shaping" was another Wyeth innovation, in which the newly cut blocks were trimmed by a kind of iron plane as they were put into the icehouse). An additional cost to the industry was the hay, tan, chaff, and sawdust used for insulating the ice.

The sawdust was brought from the timber mills of Maine in fleets of ships at an annual cost of sixteen thousand dollars.

Despite the problems with carting the ice, the Boston ice trade had almost doubled in three years, from 18,700 tons exported in 1837 to 32,297 tons, carried in 140 different vessels, in 1840. The promoters boasted:

> this is sent to the *EAST INDIES, BRAZILS, NEW SOUTH WALES, JAMAICA, CUBA, MARTINIQUE, NEW ORLEANS, MOBILE, NATCHES* [sic], *CHARLESTON* and many other ports, and will command a market in every seaport in both the Indies. In many of these ports it is sold to all classes including the *slaves* and the consumption has in all cases rapidly increased with every diminution of the price.

This is the first mention of ice being sent to Australia, although there is no evidence that Frederic Tudor or Nathaniel Wyeth shipped it there. Quite often in the following decades there are references to ice going to China, to New Zealand, and all other corners of the globe where there might have been a demand, but no details are given of the ships or the shippers. It is likely that these cargoes were irregular, just ice as a form of ballast, and that whatever market there was for them did not compare with those that became established in India, which soon after the Calcutta trade began included Bombay and Madras, where the British communities obliged by building icehouses.

Ice was certainly shipped to Peru, for in his memoirs *Old Sailing Ship Days* John Whidden recalls the time his ship the *Revere* ran aground on the treacherous shores of Tierra del

Fuego, on the southern tip of South America, with a hold full of ice and timber stacked between the decks. The crew managed to get the ship afloat and they made for the Falkland Islands to repair the damaged hull. Safe in Port Stanley, they were able to sell the timber, but the ice had no value on an island close to the Antarctic and inhabited by penguins: "Having disposed of our lumber at a good price to 'Dean & Co' the only mercantile house in the port, we hoisted the cakes of ice, dumping them in the harbor until the waters around the ship looked like a small section of the Arctic Ocean!" That was in 1851, when ice was being delivered regularly to the gold diggers of San Francisco in ships that had to navigate the treacherous waters of Cape Horn.

Wyeth and his partners won the right to have the Charlestown railroad extended to Fresh Pond and Spy Pond, and found the financial backing to get it built. The first trainload of ice left Fresh Pond for Charlestown wharf in December 1841 in specially insulated trucks designed by Wyeth. The steam trains brought a new hazard to the timber icehouses, for they belched sparks as well as vapor, and there was a danger of fire. Extra storage space was needed to hold the stocks for the rising summer demand, and Wyeth bought into the local brick-making business to provide the materials for a brick icehouse. It was the largest that had ever been built, with a holding capacity of forty thousand tons. The double-cavity walls were three feet thick and it was filled in winter by means of a horse-driven conveyor-belt system patented by Wyeth.

All in all, the apportioning of ownership of ponds, the building of the railroad, and the enormous storage capacity of the icehouses raised property values where ice was harvested.

Ice-cutting rights could be leased if the owners did not want to take out the ice themselves.

Frederic Tudor benefited greatly from all this. Although he was still paying off his coffee debts, he was earning enough in the early 1840s to live well at the same time. He began a program of tree planting on Nahant, and bought a fine town house in Boston for his wife, Effie, and their firstborn, a girl named Euphemia, after her mother, and nicknamed Effita by Frederic. He greatly enjoyed fatherhood, and his young wife complained that he remained sexually vigorous and demanding in his mid-fifties. With all his activities both as a family man and as the new squire of Nahant, Frederic might have been expected to mellow a little in his business affairs. But he did not. In these years, while remaining very successful in the ice trade, he fell out with three of the people who over the years had helped him more than anybody else to survive when the going was tough.

Frederic's brother-in-law Robert Gardiner, married to his sister Emma, suffered a disastrous fire on his estate on the Kennebec River and saw his fortune dwindle away. He turned to Frederic for help, and managed to persuade the man whose life he had helped to save twenty years earlier to lend him just over a thousand dollars. Frederic, who had spent the whole of his earlier career in debt to innumerable creditors, was not pleased to learn that Gardiner had borrowed more money without first paying him back. Then came a bombshell. Emma, writing in 1839 to a family friend who had asked about the origins of the ice trade, retold the family story: though Frederic had made it a success, it was William who first had the idea of exporting ice to the West Indies. Though Robert had nothing to do with this,

Frederic cut off all ties with him and the Gardiner family, and refused them any further financial help.

At the same time, Frederic began a long and costly dispute with his icehouse keeper in Havana, the long-serving and faithful carpenter John Damon, who had worked for him longer than anybody else. Damon felt that he should be better rewarded for sticking it out in Cuba, an island Frederic had not visited for years and had come to dislike heartily. Frederic accused Damon of cheating him, and tried to replace him. This disagreement became known as the "Havana Ice House Controversy," with Damon protesting his case and his innocence in a privately published pamphlet, and Frederic dismissing him as a scoundrel. Whatever the rights and wrongs of the dispute, Damon did not repay Frederic any money, and set up in business on his own. The episode cut back Frederic's profits and delayed the day when he could pay off his coffee debts.

One man with whom Frederic might have been expected to remain on good terms was Nathaniel Wyeth, but he managed to poison that relationship as well. The source of the disagreement was quite bizarre, and is ultimately inexplicable. When Wyeth had gone to Oregon for the first time in 1832, he had handed his patent on the ice plow to Frederic as surety on a loan. Now back in the ice business, Wyeth wanted to enforce the patent, which he believed that a rival harvester on Fresh Pond had stolen.

When the case was heard in 1840, the defendant argued that the ice plow was no different from a carpenter's plow plane, and in any case, Wyeth had not tried to enforce his 1829 patent for ten years even though he knew others were using ice plows similar to his own. After much deliberation, the judgment was that Wyeth's patent was valid, and that he had not abandoned his right to it by allowing others to use it. But there was the question of Frederic's interest in the patent. This had never been formally registered—it was just an agreement that had been made between the two when Frederic gave Wyeth his loan—but it was necessary for Frederic to back Wyeth's claim. He refused to do so, and the case was lost on this technicality. Why he behaved in this way is a mystery.

There were further rebuffs to Wyeth before he broke away in 1846 to run his own ice business. After the Charlestown railway was extended to Fresh Pond, the citizens of Fitchburg, a town farther inland, successfully petitioned for it to be extended to them. This took the railroad past the town of Concord and close to the shores of Walden Pond, which until that time had not been exploited for Boston's ice trade, as it was too far from the port to be commercially useful. Right away, Frederic bought harvesting rights on Walden Pond, and in the winter of 1846–47 sent a team to cut a few thousand tons of ice and stack it on the shore. The wagons that then brought the Walden ice to Charlestown thundered past Fresh Pond, where Wyeth was hard at work filling his vast brick icehouse. This episode was hurtful to Wyeth, but it gave rise to the most celebrated account of the emergence of the ice trade as a hugely efficient industry capable of exporting ice around the world.

It so happened that at the time Frederic sent his team of ice harvesters to exploit Walden Pond, a young man whose family home was in Concord, close by, had built himself a log cabin on the shore as a kind of retreat from the bustle of town life. He was Henry David Thoreau, then twenty-eight years old and an aspiring literary figure from a town that boasted such luminaries as the poet and essayist Ralph Waldo Emerson. Thoreau's father had been a farmer, then the owner of a grocery store in Boston, and had returned to Concord to take over his brother-in-law's pencil factory. Henry received a private education and studied at Harvard, where he met up with a group of intellectuals known as transcendentalists, who believed in the spiritual unity of the world and the power of the "spirit" over reason. They were forerunners in some ways of the contemporary green movements that oppose genetic engineering and agribusiness. Though his education was paid for by his father's business, and he worked in it himself at times, Thoreau was opposed to what he regarded as "modernization" and "commercialization" in and around Concord.

At the time the railway and then Frederic's ice harvesters arrived, Thoreau was at work in his log cabin on his most famous book, which he called simply *Walden*. It is an eccentric work in which he attempts to derive some deep philosophical meaning from his observation of the minutiae of daily life around Walden Pond. He describes, for example, the local farmers coming to cut ice there in winter and inviting him to join in. They are a jolly lot, and joke with him that he might like to help cut the ice "pitsaw fashion," with him underneath (when cutting timber planks, one man would be underneath in the pit, and another above). If they were cutting ice, this meant Thoreau would be underwater. These rustic ice cutters to him represented a pleasingly local enterprise—in sharp contrast to Frederic's men, who were taking advantage of the new railroad, which Thoreau regarded as a destructive influence, drawing life out of Concord and dispatching it to Boston.

Thoreau found the whole idea of the commercial harvesting of ice absurd, and he struggled to find words to describe what he saw with his own eyes from his log cabin in the winter of 1846–47. First, in his chapter on "The Pond in Winter," he tries fantasy:

> . . . there came a hundred men of Hyperborean extraction swoop down on to our pond one morning, with many carloads of ungainly looking farming tools, sleds, ploughs, drill-barrows, turf-knives, spades, saws, rakes and each man was armed with a double-pointed pike-staff such as is not described in the New England Farmer or Cultivator. I did not know whether they had come to sow a crop of winter rye, or some other kind of grain recently introduced from Iceland. As I saw no manure, I judged that they meant to skim the land, as I had done, thinking the soil was deep and had lain fallow long enough. They said that a gentleman farmer, who was behind the scenes, wanted to double his money, which, as I understood, amounted to half a million already.

Thoreau, of course, knew exactly what these men were doing and who the millionaire farmer was, for he mentioned Tudor in a letter to Emerson. His account continued:

> To speak literally, a hundred Irishmen, with Yankee overseers, came from Cambridge every day to get out the ice. They divided it into cakes by methods too well known to require description, and these, being sledded to the shore were rapidly hauled off on to an ice platform, and raised by grappling irons and block and tackle, worked by horses, onto a stack, as surely as so many barrels of flour, and there placed evenly side by side, and row upon row, as they formed the solid base of an obelisk designed to pierce the clouds.

There were no icehouses at Walden Pond, and Thoreau describes the great stack covered in hay and boards looking like "a venerable moss-grown, hoary ruin, built of azure tinted marble, the abode of Winter, that old man we see in the almanac." Some of the ice was hauled away, but much was left until the summer. In July, more was taken from the stack, but a considerable quantity was simply left to melt away without any hay or boards to insulate it. Thoreau recorded that it had not quite all melted by September 1848.

> Ice is an interesting subject for contemplation. They told me that they had some in the ice-houses at Fresh Pond five years old which was as good as ever. Why is it that a bucket of water soon becomes putrid, but frozen remains sweet forever? . . . Thus for sixteen days I saw from my window a hundred men at work like busy husbandmen, with teams and horses and apparently all the implements of farming . . . and now they are all gone and in thirty days more, probably, I shall look from the same window on the pure sea-green Walden water there . . . and no traces will appear that man has ever stood there.

Thoreau had been reading classic Indian texts, popular with transcendentalists, and he found it amusing that water from the lake in which he might take a dip in summer was sent frozen to India: "The pure Walden water is mingled with the sacred water of the Ganges."

Walden was published in 1856 to a resounding lack of interest, and it was not until after Thoreau's death in 1862 that it was reevaluated as a classic anti-industrial text, featuring Frederic's opportunistic exploitation of Walden Pond. Whereas Thoreau spurned riches and regarded such innovations as the electric telegraph, railroads, and refrigeration as destructive, Frederic simply wanted to be rich so that he could enjoy whatever benefits modernization might bring to Boston. And by 1849 the rapid growth in the ice trade, of which the Walden Pond episode was a symptom, finally enabled Frederic to fulfill his dream of solvency and real, untrammeled wealth.

In that year, Wyeth contributed a piece on "The Ice Trade of the United States" to *The American Almanac and Repository of Useful Knowledge*. While giving credit to Tudor as the pioneer of the trade, in his typically self-effacing manner, Wyeth listed without attribution all the great innovations, the majority of which were his own. Most of the machinery for stacking ice blocks in the stores was still horse drawn, and all the cutting was done with horse-drawn cutters, but the industry had grown to such an extent that, as Wyeth wrote, "more ice is now secured in one favorable day than would have supplied the whole trade in 1832." Although the ice trade was growing fast in New York, Philadelphia, Baltimore, Washington, and other cities, Wyeth does not produce any figures for these places, perhaps because by "ice trade" he meant the export business, which was still almost exclusively Boston-based.

The scale of operations was impressive. In 1847, nearly 52,000 tons of ice was shipped down the coast to twenty-eight different towns. To the established markets in New Orleans, Charleston, and Savannah were added Washington, D.C., Philadelphia, Mobile (Alabama), Key West (Florida), Norfolk (Virginia), and twenty more. In this one year, 258 vessels carried ice in this coast-long trade, and about 23,000 tons were carried in 95 ships to foreign ports. As well as Calcutta, Madras, and Bombay, cargoes were sent to more than half a dozen West Indian islands, Hong Kong, Ceylon, Whampoa (China), Rio de Janeiro, Batavia (now Jakarta), and three Cuban ports, making thirty-one foreign destinations in all. At the end of the list is the English port of Liverpool. Wyeth himself had taken up the trade Tudor had dabbled in, sending, packed in ice, fruit and other perishables to the West Indies. In 1849, he says twenty-nine cargoes of provisions were shipped to ports "where otherwise such articles could not be sent," and includes in his list Barbados, Trinidad, Demerara, Antigua, St. Vincent, Guadeloupe, St. Thomas, Honduras, and Calcutta. As insulation for the ice and the food cargoes, 4,600 cords of sawdust, which had proved to be the most effective material to spread between and around blocks of ice, were shipped to Boston from the lumber mills of Maine. Before the ice trade, Maine sawdust had been worthless and often accumulated in rivers, damming them and causing flooding. Now it was sold at $2.50 a cord to the Boston ice merchants.

In the summer months, there were now regular deliveries of ice to people living in Boston and the surrounding districts. More than sixty horse-drawn wagons picked up supplies either from the Charlestown railway depot or directly from the icehouses on the shores of Fresh Pond, Spy Pond, and other bodies of water where ice was harvested to satisfy local demand. At 27,000 tons in 1847, Boston ice consumption had outstripped the total export trade. The problem of a poor harvest in a mild winter had more or less been solved by the enormous storage capacity of the icehouses. On the shores of Fresh Pond alone there was now capacity for 86,732 tons of ice, and supplies from a good year could last through to the next season. (Walden Pond is not mentioned, for it appears to have been visited only occasionally by the ice harvesters.)

Frederic Tudor was now just one ice merchant among many, but the growth of the trade was such that by the beginning of 1849, he had paid off his entire coffee debt, which with interest amounted to $280,000. At the same time he had become wealthy almost by accident, for the largest part of his fortune was now in property rather than direct profits from the ice trade, though that provided him with a considerable annual income of around forty thousand dollars. He made no public announcement of his hard-won solvency. Instead, he wrote a letter, dated January 22, 1849, to the agent of his major creditor, a Mr. Wiggin, setting out his position. Like all Frederic's correspondence, this was not simply a business letter: he was far too emotional for that. It is an account of his struggle for survival, and a note at the end says that the letter should be placed in the files of the Massachusetts Historical Society, but not published until after his death. In other words, he was writing for posterity.

How had he done it? First, Frederic pays tribute to the British communities in India, who he says appreciated his policy of selling ice at a reasonable price:

> This policy of cheap selling was met by the English inhabitants of Calcutta, with the most open handed and generous liberality. They made me a subscription and a present of a fine fire proof building *unconditionally* and this example was followed nearly in the same way at Madras and Bombay. All these things strengthened me.

There was a steady demand for ice in Calcutta, but the trade did not increase greatly, confined as it was to the English community there: "For the natives it was a nine days wonder," wrote Tudor. It was the trade with the southern states, and New Orleans in particular, that grew rapidly after 1835:

> For several years a single cargo would supply New Orleans and the same in Charleston S.C. But the demand rapidly and suddenly increased, in those two places, particularly in New Orleans, when I have now to ship thirty cargoes and a like quantity is shipped by others.

To keep up with the demand, he had to buy land for new "depositories" in the ports where ice was delivered. By 1849, he had five sites in New Orleans, a large one in Charleston, a brick ice store in Kingston, Jamaica, and others in many places around the world. Once the right to harvest ice on Fresh Pond was made dependent on the ownership of shoreline, Frederic had to invest a good deal of his profits acquiring lakeside land. He bought 158 acres and two houses at Fresh Pond, and smaller amounts of shoreline land at Spot Pond, Walden Pond, and Smith Pond. In answer to complaints that he had been over-investing when he was heavily in debt, he answered that he was forced to buy harvesting rights:

> They may be likened to the seed, necessary to the harvest. If the purchase of them had not been made, the business could not have been continued . . . The ice trade from contempt and derision began to grow most rapidly and if I had not secured the several Ponds and lands on their Banks, at the moment I did, I should have in all probability

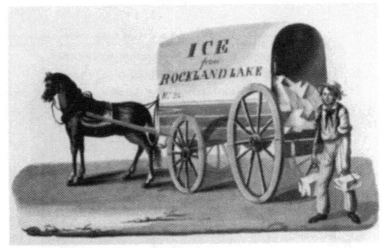

Regular deliveries of lake and river ice began in New York in the 1840s. A favorite source was Rockland Lake, which was known for the purity of its water—though much of the ice sold under that name would have come from the Hudson River, which in later years was lined with huge ice storehouses.

Ice on Jamaica Pond, marked out by horse-drawn ice ploughs, ready for breaking off and storing in huge wooden warehouses. The elevator taking the ice to the top of the warehouse—loading was from the top—is worked by a steam engine housed in the wooden shed. Sparks from these engines and from trains often set the warehouses on fire: When the timber had burned away, a huge mass of congealed and sooty ice would be left.

Although they look primitive, a great deal of thought went into the design of refrigerators, or ice-boxes. They were troublesome, with melt-water continually drained off, and often gave off an unpleasant smell. This "air dry box" was patented in 1882.

Above A classic image of American icemen making domestic deliveries in Boston. The blocks carried with tongs were a regulation size to fit household refrigerators. Jamaica Pond, Boston, was just one of the many clear-water lakes which gave a winter harvest of ice.

Right One of a huge variety of domestic freezers marketed in the United States and Britain from the mid-nineteenth century. Although it was advertised as an "ice making" machine it was no such thing. To make ice cream a "freezing mixture" of salt and ice was needed, which by chemical reaction drew heat from the ice-cream mixture, an ancient devise used by Tudor to make the first ice creams in Martinique.

The practical working of the same is shown daily at the **ATMOSPHERIC CHURN COMPANY,** 119, NEW BOND STREET.

The interior of one of the giant wooden ice-houses built along the Kennebec River in Maine to supply the growing demand for ice in New York, Washington, Philadelphia, and Baltimore from the 1870s. Techniques for stacking the ice cubes and discharging them into sailing ships were sophisticated, requiring many now long-forgotten skills.

Ice harvesting on the Kennebec River. As the demand for ice rose further south and milder winters brought regular "ice famines," the Kennebec became the major supplier to east coast cities, whose ice companies bought harvesting rights on the river. This huge timber ice-house at Cedar Grove was owned by the Cochran-Oler Ice company of Baltimore.

The Kennebec harvest of 1889, with "canalmen" breaking off huge blocks of ice, much of it destined for New York. To the right of the elevator house is slush ice which has been scooped from the surface before marking and cutting; to the left is waste ice from "planing off" the blocks to remove dirt before they were stored. Some of this harvest would end up in popular drinks such as "cobblers" and "smashes," in which crushed ice was mixed with liqueurs and fruit juices.

When demand was high because of a warm winter further south the Kennebec harvesters could cut and store several million tons of ice in a few weeks. Here a steam-driven continuous elevator scoops up the ice blocks as they are coaxed into position along a free-water canal.

One of a number of steam-driven artificial ice-making machines which were built to compete with the harvests of natural ice. This one was on show at an international exhibition in 1882. Around that time such machines put an end to the frozen-water trade with India, but they could not compete on price or quantity in North America for another twenty-five years.

Frederic Tudor still looking defiant in his distinguished and prosperous old age, when he spent most of his time at his country estate on the island of Nahant, a popular resort for Bostonians. He died a wealthy man in 1864, at the age of eighty.

Euphemia Fenno married Tudor in 1834, when he was nearly fifty and she thirty years younger. They had six children, but after Frederic's death she angrily scribbled some notes in one of his diaries which indicated that he had kept a mistress, a lover he had had since before they married.

Frederic Tudor's last project was the creation on his Nahant estate of Maolis Gardens of an amusement park with an entrance fee of five cents for adults and three cents for children. There was an ice-cream pavilion and "cool soda" was served. Natural ice provided the refrigeration.

A business card of the Knickerbocker Ice Company of Philadelphia, which in 1890 was offering customers daily deliveries of between five and a hundred tons of ice for a weekly payment. Its ice depots are listed and it offers to supply customers in Camden, Atlantic City, and Cape May, New Jersey. On the reverse of the card the same company offers to supply coal in winter from horse-drawn wagons.

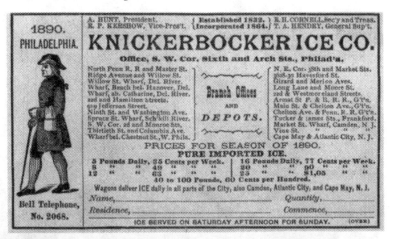

Although in the mid-nineteenth century Massachusetts ice was shipped to England and was briefly fashionable, Norway, borrowing American techniques, could undercut the Atlantic trade. From lakes close to the sea ice was shipped to the east coast and London from the 1850s to the 1920s, chiefly to commercial buyers such as fishmongers.

The Norway ice trade never matched that of America. Some idea of the relative scale of operations is given by this photograph of a block of Norway ice being unloaded from a ship docked at Great Yarmouth in Norfolk.

been cut off from my means of supply of Ice, now amounting on the average to 60 cargoes annually as others have taken up the business extensively.

Whereas the value of Frederic's vast holdings of coffee had fallen disastrously, everything he had acquired in pursuit of the ice trade had risen markedly in value:

> Ice now goes from Boston in a very large way . . . Rail Roads have been built (one of them solely for the transport of ice), water on the shores of Ponds is now leased and is nearly as valuable in convenient localities as the land itself. The astonishing growth of Boston, now the center of four cities in consequence of the Rail Roads, has caused these lands, which I have purchased, to rise in value.

Frederic had bought land at Fresh Pond for $130 an acre and at Spot Pond for $80. In his letter, he says he has been offered $2,000 an acre for part of his Fresh Pond holding, and that recently land had sold at Spot Pond for $800 an acre: "I have the satisfaction to see without having so intended I have been gaining the means of being comfortable and well off in my elder period of life and that I shall not leave my family and children penniless."

Frederic was sixty-five years old when he wrote this letter. He suffered a little from lumbago, but he was still vigorous and still very much involved in the ice trade, though he had tried to find someone to manage his business for him. There were now four children: Effie; Frederic, his first son, born in 1845; Delia, born in 1847; and William, born in 1848. He had begun to worry about what would happen to his family if he should die. But his last years were to be the happiest and most satisfying of his adult life, as he developed his estate at Nahant and basked in the praise he was to receive for creating an entirely new and very American social habit, the wholesale consumption of ice.

10

Wenham Lake

B y the time Frederic had paid off his coffee debt, European visitors to Boston, New York, and other cities on the eastern seaboard of the United States could not fail to notice that in summer there was an awful lot of ice around, and that what was still a rarity and a great luxury on the other side of the Atlantic was considered to be an essential comfort in America. In the streets, there were the ice carts delivering to hotels and homes, the icemen familiar figures as they hoisted perspiring chunks of crystal up staircases and into doorways with their iron tongs. Water was almost always drunk chilled, and there were many drinks that had crushed ice as an essential ingredient, such as sherry cobblers or mint juleps. Just as Frederic had predicted, once people had tried chilled drinks, they were hooked, and would no longer tolerate tepid water. He had proved his point in Havana, in the American south, and in India, and now all Americans who had to endure sweltering summers had caught the ice habit. But not even Frederic could have anticipated just how widespread the use of ice would become in America.

One of the best of the many accounts of the pleasures of ice in America is in a travelogue written by a middle-aged English-woman, Sarah Mytton Maury, who with her doctor toured the eastern seaboard in the 1840s to give herself a much-needed break from years of childbearing. She wrote:

> . . . of all the luxuries in America I most enjoyed the ice—its use was then rare and expensive in England; it was a luxury only indulged in on occasions of company and display, but among the middle classes it was unknown as an article of domestic and daily luxury. Even now its use is chiefly confined to the Metropolis, where it is provided to the grateful inhabitants at the rate of three to four cents a pound. ("Wenham Lake Ice" is painted on the cart which conveys it from door to door.) I found it a most refreshing practice to place several jugs of iced water in my bedroom during the great heats; the atmosphere became perceptibly cooled. It is customary when you pay a visit, for the attendant immediately on your arrival to present you with iced water or iced lemonade. I have also a most grateful memory of various houses, where after a heated and dusty drive or walk, I was ushered into an apartment from which the light and air having been carefully excluded (chiefly by outside green shutters) the relief on entering was indescribably pleasant and the ice water a perfect luxury.

Mrs. Maury invites her readers to a "typical" dinner party in New York, which begins with champagne served with two chunks of ice the "size of walnuts," with which "animating and cool" beverage she proposes a toast to the memory of the Old

Country and the prospects of the New. After turtle soup, oyster pie, and a variety of poultry, ice cream and chilled fruits are served, and there is iced milk and iced water on the table. American hosts, she wrote, were very proud of their ice, which they regarded as a mark of civilization that put them ahead of their European cousins: " 'Whenever you hear America abused' observed a lady to me as she presented a glass of sparkling Sherry cobbler, with the huge crystals floating about in the exquisitely co-mingled cup, 'remember the ice.' "

The sherry cobblers Mrs. Maury so enjoyed were made up of wine or liqueur, fruit, and sugar, with a good helping of crushed or broken ice. She was amused to learn that her hosts claimed that not all ice was of the same quality: "It was curious to hear the Americans occasionally find fault with the flavour of ice. 'Come and taste the ice from my pond at Forest Hill,' said some fastidious and abstemious Guardian, one day at Coleman's 'and you will then perceive what inferior stuff this is.' "

In reality, most American consumers, living far from the source of their ice, had little idea where it came from or how it was harvested, though the supplier might claim that his source was the very best. For example, in New York, the wagons of the Rockland Lake Ice Company were all over town, giving customers the impression that they were getting clear, frozen water from the mountains to the north. Rockland Lake was indeed a major source of ice, but so were many other lakes and rivers, and distributors in New York would buy from any of these. A great deal came from the Hudson River, although it was not sold as such.

The British in India were even less likely to have any notion of the origin of the ice that arrived on the Hooghly in American ships. However, in the mid-century, exported American ice acquired a trade name and was known ever after as "Wenham Lake Ice." This gave rise to the belief that there was a single source of ice in America—a stretch of water that had quite exceptional qualities of purity and durability when frozen. In fact, the only difference between ice from Wenham Lake, near Salem, Massachusetts, and any other frozen water from New England was the way in which it was marketed.

The story of Wenham's international fame began with the first attempts to sell Massachusetts ice in England. One of Frederic Tudor's competitors who had harvesting rights on Fresh Pond thought London must be a great untapped market, especially as English visitors to America were so enthusiastic about the chilled drinks and ice cream they could not enjoy at home. Jacob Hittinger, of the newly formed ice merchants Gage, Hittinger & Co., dispatched his first cargo of ice from Fresh Pond to London in 1842. At more or less the same time, a wealthy young man named Charles B. Lander, who lived in Salem, the seaport to the north of Boston, decided that the ice business was worth a try. The nearest source of supply was Wenham Lake, and Lander bought some shoreline and put up icehouses. A railway to Boston Harbor ran close to the lake, making the transport of the ice straightforward. Anybody with the will and the resources could now set up an ice business in no time, for all the technological problems had been solved.

While the brig *Sharon* carried Jacob Hittinger's Fresh Pond ice to London, Hittinger himself went on ahead in one of the new transatlantic steamers to make arrangements for promoting it. Taking a leaf out of Frederic Tudor's book, the first thing he did when his ice arrived in London was to hire some bartenders and teach them to make chilled American drinks—juleps, cobblers, smashes, and other cocktails. He advertised the ice's arrival in the *Times,* but there was not much interest: as he put it when he told the story more than thirty years later to *Scribner's* magazine, "it seemed to them a strange fish that no one dared to touch":

> My feelings were just about the temperature of my ice and wasting as rapidly. At last I was introduced to the Chairman or President of the Fishmongers Association, an association which I was not long in discovering had the merit of wealth, if not of social position. He was sociable and seemed to comprehend my position if I didn't his.
>
> Matters were soon arranged; a magnificent hall or saloon had been secured; I ascertained that my bar-keepers, through constant drill, had attained the correct sleight of hand in mixing the drinks. The hour arrived. The hall was long and brilliantly lighted. After the company was seated, the chairman introduced me and the subject matter of the evening's discussion. Now, thought I, I am all right. At a given signal the well-trained waiters appeared, laden with the different drinks.
>
> The effect was gorgeous, and I expected an ovation that no Yankee had ever had. But, alas! The first sounds that broke the silence were "I say—aw, waitaw, a little 'ot wataw if you please; I prefer it 'alf and 'alf." I made a dead rush for the door, next day settled my bills in London, took the train for Liverpool and the steamer for Boston, and counted up a clear loss of $1,200.

Hittinger came to the conclusion that there was no call for chilled drinks in England, and never tried to sell ice there again.

However, Charles B. Lander was determined to try to open up this potentially profitable market. He had caused a good deal of resentment around Lake Wenham by putting up one of his icehouses on a hillock known locally as Peter's Pulpit, in commemoration of a fiery sermon preached there in 1642, and his moving of the old Wenham meetinghouse to the shore of the lake to use as an ice depository was not popular either. Before he had harvested any ice, Lander ran short of money, and had to bring in new partners. But by June 1844, he had a ship, the *Ellen*, loaded with a thousand tons of ice and en route to Liverpool.

Lander went on ahead in a steamer to begin his promotional campaign, opening offices in Liverpool and some other provincial cities, but most successfully in London. He advertised his ice as "Concentrated Wenham"—"concentrated *venom*" in the Cockney accent of the time, inspiring the satirical magazine *Punch*, which had great fun with the whole episode, to suggest it was poisonous. Lander's great publicity coup was to put a block of ice in the window of the Wenham Lake Ice Company's office in The Strand. This became a sensation. Londoners could not understand how a block of ice could stay there all day without melting, and many even doubted that it was really ice. Passersby would ask if they could touch it, and wondered at the frozen fish that sometimes appeared in the middle of the blocks, which were so clear you could read a newspaper right through them. Henry Colman, a New Englander in London in 1845, was much amused by the Yankee ploy that so baffled the English. In his *European Life and Manners*, published in 1849, he wrote:

I am reminded of Salem whenever I go down the Strand, by the sign of the Wenham Lake Ice Company, and a large block of ice which appears at the window. In passing the shop, the other day, on the box of an omnibus, I heard a very well-dressed person, who sat on the other side of the driver, gravely inform him that this ice came from the West Indies; very marvelous geographical knowledge!

This block of ice is about eighteen inches square, and about twelve thick. The Londoners look upon it in amazement. I am told they sometimes go into the shop after gazing through the window, and put their hands on it, to be sure that it is not glass. Many consider it likewise, a sort of standing miracle, for they don't see that it diminishes, not having a suspicion that the cunning Yankee who exhibits it, takes a new piece out of the refrigerator every morning.

By "refrigerator," Colman meant simply the ice store in The Strand.

The Wenham Lake Ice Company attempted to establish in London the kind of delivery system that was common in America, whereby householders were encouraged to buy iceboxes that could be kept perpetually cool in the summer with a regular supply of ice. Horse-drawn vans left the main store in The Strand twice a day, at 8 A.M. and 3 P.M., and customers were asked to put in their orders an hour ahead of these times. The delivery men wore uniforms on which were sewn specially designed buttons displaying an American eagle clutching an olive branch in one talon and five arrows in the other. On the eagle's breast was a small shield with the Massachusetts seal, a "Red Indian" with bow and arrow surmounted by a bent arm and a gauntleted hand gripping a sword. Queen Victoria and

Prince Albert were among those who developed a taste for Wenham ice, and the company became suppliers "by appointment" to Her Majesty.

English magazines like *Punch* enjoyed many speculations on the possible uses of Wenham ice, such as paving the capital's streets with something less slippery than wood, or turning the Serpentine in Hyde Park into a skating rink. On May 17, 1845, the *Illustrated London News* published a long article about the origins of the ice, illustrated with a sketch of ice harvesting at Wenham Lake based on information supplied by the company, which seems to have provided the newspaper with all its facts and figures. The article must have greatly amused any New Englander who read it. For example:

> One surprising circumstance connected with the trade, is the fact that their Ice, though transported to this country in the heat of the summer, is not reduced in bulk. Those engaged in the trade, we find, account for this by the fact that the masses of Ice are so large that they expose a very small surface to atmospheric action in proportion to their weight, and therefore do not suffer from exposure to it as the smaller and thinner fragments do, which are obtained in our own or other warmer climates.

In other words, Wenham ice was not just any old frozen water—it had unique lasting properties. While it is true that large blocks of ice last longer in temperatures above zero than smaller ones, they would not have survived a sea voyage of a month, never mind storage on the shores of Wenham Lake from March until June, unless they were well insulated. And though Wyeth's ice plow had greatly improved the efficiency of the trade by producing neat squares or rectangles of ice, Frederic Tudor had successfully exported roughly cut ice for twenty years before the ice plow was in use.

More to the point about American ice was its apparent cleanliness, another quality stressed in the *Illustrated London News*:

> The peculiar and ascertained purity of the Ice used in America, fits it for table-use; and it is accordingly the constant custom there to mix it with water or milk, for drinking; to dilute it with wines or spirits, and to place it upon the table, in direct contact with butter and jellies. Some of our hotels and taverns are beginning to use this Ice for the manufacture of Mint-juleps and Sherry-cobblers, and other American beverages of celebrity; and we should not be surprised if these tempting drinks, as well as the Ice itself, were to come into very general use.

A month later the *European and Liverpool Times* expressed a similar view. It had its own theory about the extraordinary chilling properties of this very special commodity:

> A particle dropped in a beaker of claret instantly reduces the temperature of that beverage without the least deteriorating its quality, a result wholly unobtainable by the substitution of English ice, of which six times the bulk is required to produce the same effect as the expulsion of caloric, which latter ice is really equivalent to a dilution by just so many times as spring water. In the cooling of fruit, jellies, confections and the like, and even the cooling of large crowded rooms, by placing a block of the Wenham Lake ice in a passage where a current of air can pass over it, is also considered invaluable.

This pseudoscientific nonsense aroused the interest of Sir Charles Lyell, the eminent geologist and mentor of Charles Darwin, who made a detour to the lake when he was visiting New England in 1846. "The water is clear and pure and the bottom covered with white quartz-rose sand," he noted in his travelogue *A Second Visit to the United States of North America* (1849). "It is fed by springs and receives no mud from any spring flowing into it." Lyell reported that the famous scientist Michael Faraday, who had conducted experiments with artificial refrigeration, had examined Wenham ice and found it "exceedingly pure, being both free from air-bubbles and from salts." Lyell conducted an experiment to compare Wenham ice and English ice:

> The presence of the first [i.e., air bubbles] makes it extremely difficult to succeed in making a lens of English ice which will concentrate the solar rays and readily fire gunpowder, whereas nothing is easier than to perform this singular feat of igniting a combustible body by the aid of a frozen mass, if Wenham ice is employed.

Whereas others believed North American ice, and that from Wenham Lake in particular, lasted longer than English ice because it started out colder, Sir Charles rejected this on the grounds that once it was exposed to temperatures above freezing, ice was bound to melt, however frozen it was in the first place. He felt that it was the "impurities" in English ice that made it melt quicker. Strangely, he does not mention insulation, which was the real key to keeping and transporting ice.

What seems to have impressed the English most was that, according to the *European and Liverpool Times*, a block of

Wenham ice would hardly melt at all over a long night "in the sultriest apartment," and that its "crystal-like transparency, reflecting and refracting the lights of the chandeliers in multitudinous hues, renders it an object of general attraction."

After two seasons, it looked as if the Wenham Lake Ice Company had cracked the London market. It had established a delivery system, and wooden refrigerators were advertised for sale in the *Times* and other newspapers. The *European and Liverpool Times* reported that Wenham ice had become an essential feature of all grand dinners in London. So fashionable was it that William Thackeray in his satirical story "A Little Dinner at Timmins's" (1856) treated it as a cliché:

> As for describing, then, the mere victuals on Timmins table, that would be absurd. Everybody—(I mean the genteel world of course, of which I make no doubt the reader is a polite ornament)—Everybody has the same everything in London. You see the same coats, the same dinners, the same boiled fowls and mutton, the same cutlets, fish and cucumbers, the same lumps of Wenham Lake ice etc. . . . Can't anyone invent anything new?

In fact, the taste for Wenham ice in London turned out to be just a passing fad. Refrigerators did not catch on even in the best households, as they had done in America and in India. As late as the 1930s, Londoners were still surprised by the American liking for cold drinks, and though the well-to-do might have ice in their cellars in the summer to keep food fresh, they never thought of actually consuming it. Englishmen drank their beer warm, and GIs who were sent to Europe during the Second World War had to be warned in informational films that they could not expect cold beer or ice in their drinks, as they had back home.

Just how far behind America London was in getting the ice habit is graphically revealed by the chronicler of the capital's mid-nineteenth-century life, the journalist Henry Mayhew. Among his portraits of street life published in the *Morning Chronicle* and later collected in *London Labour and the London Poor* is an interview with one of the first ice cream sellers, who plied his trade around 1851:

> Yes, sir, I mind very well the first time as I ever sold ices. I don't think they'll ever take greatly in the streets, but there's no saying. Lord! How I've seen the people splutter when they've tasted them for the first time. I did as much myself. They get among the teeth and make you feel as you tooth-ached all over. I sold mostly strawberry ices. I haven't an idea how they're made, but it's a most wonderful thing in summer—freezing fruits in that way. One young Irish fellow—I think from his look and cap he was a printer's or stationer's boy—he bought an ice off me and when he had scraped it all together with the spoon, he made a pull at it as if he was a drinking beer. In course it was all among his teeth in less than no time, and he stood like a stattey [statue] for a instant, and then he roared out: "Jasus. I'm kilt. The could [cold] shivers is on me!"

There was, however, a taste for ice cream in the wealthiest families, and the ice cream seller went on to say that the maids and grooms from the big houses seemed to know how to eat it without fearing for their lives.

Later in the century, ice cream became more widely popular. It was bought on the street or in ice cream parlors, but was rarely made at home because few people had a refrigerator or anywhere to store ice. Even in the 1920s, when the Walls Company started making ice creams as a summer sideline to its sausage business, they were sold by men riding tricycles equipped with dry iceboxes, as few shops, let alone homes, had refrigerators. For many years, the slogan was "Stop me and buy one!"

The Wenham Lake Ice Company ultimately failed to convert the English public to an essentially American custom and abandoned the attempt after a few years. The only profitable market for ice was commercial: it was in demand by the big manufacturers of ice cream, such as the Italian Carlo Gatti,* and as a preservative for fish, meat, and milk. From 1850, it was the Norwegians, with abundant good-quality natural ice that could be cut close to the fjords near Oslo, who took over the industrial ice trade with England. They copied the American industry, having in the 1840s sent representatives to New York to see how it worked. As Norway was much closer to England, the Americans could not compete on price. In any case, the quantities sent to England were tiny compared with those consumed by the burgeoning American trade. In 1850, Norway exported only 2,960 tons of ice, and even at the peak of the trade, in 1900, England bought less than half a million tons, barely enough to keep New York cool for a few weeks in the summer.

---

*Gatti (1817 to 1878) was one of the first ice cream sellers in London. He obtained his ice from the Regents Canal and later from Norway.

After Wenham Lake ice disappeared from England, it was sold exclusively in America, although its name had no special cachet there. But the idea that all American ice came from Wenham Lake had been firmly planted in British minds, and it was not long before the colonial communities in India thought it was what they were getting, though their supplier, Frederic Tudor, never harvested it.

The Norwegians, possibly irritated by constant references to this favored ice, renamed Lake Oppegaard near Oslo "Wenham Lake," thus causing further misconceptions, for Londoners had the impression that they were still receiving American ice long after supplies had ceased. Americans were amused by the confusion. The story was told in *Scribner's* magazine, which wrote up the history of the ice trade in 1875, of a Boston merchant named Thomas Groom, who on a visit to London's fish market at Billingsgate, noticed a sign that proclaimed: "Norway, London and American ice for sale." When he inquired of a fishmonger which he thought was best, he got the reply, "Oh, the London ice, sir." He asked why, and was told: "You see the American ice and the Norway ice is nothing but congealed water; it is too thick, while you see, London ice is made in one week; and being only six inches thick, is much harder than the American."

Well into the twentieth century, when ice was manufactured and the Norway trade had died away, a relative of Chad Foster Smith, who chronicled the Wenham ice story in his monograph *Crystal Blocks of Yankee Coldness,* asked a London fishmonger if he had any Wenham Lake ice and received the reply: "Why! Aven't thought o that in years. Used t'come from Norway dinit?" Others imagined that Wenham Lake, which supplied the whole world with ice, must be one of America's Great Lakes, and searched the map in vain for it.

There was the same confusion in India, where there are frequent references to Tudor's Wenham Lake ice. So famous did it become that Rudyard Kipling wove it into one of his stories. Though he was born in Bombay in 1865, when American ice was regularly delivered there, Kipling's parents left him with boarders in England when he was only six years old, and he did not go back to India until 1882, by which time the frozen-water trade had more or less ceased. However, he had heard of Wenham ice, and brought an amusing story related to it into the *Second Jungle Book,* which he wrote in the 1890s while he was living in Vermont. It is possible that the story came from his father, an artist and schoolteacher who wrote a book about men and beasts in India.

On the banks of a river in India, an Adjutant Bird, a large, storklike creature that when standing with folded wings looks like an army adjutant, is reminiscing about the past with a jackal and a mugger, a kind of crocodile:

> "When I was a bird in my third season, a young and bold bird, I went down to the river where the big boats come in. The boats of the English are thrice as big as this village."
>
> "He has been as far as Delhi and says all the people there walk on their heads," muttered the Jackal. The Mugger opened his left eye, and looked keenly at the Adjutant.
>
> "It is true," the big bird insisted. "A liar only lies when he hopes to be believed. No one who had not seen these boats could believe this truth."
>
> "That is more reasonable," said the Mugger. "And then?"
>
> "From the insides of this boat they were taking out great

pieces of white stuff, which, in a little while, turned to water. Much split off, and fell about on the shore, and the rest they swiftly put into a house with thick walls. But a boatman, who laughed, took a piece no larger than a small dog, and threw it to me. I—all my people—swallow without reflection, and that piece I swallowed as is our custom. Immediately I was afflicted with an excessive cold which, beginning in my crop, ran down to the extreme end of my toes, and deprived me even of speech, while the boatman laughed at me. Never have I felt such cold. I danced in my grief and amazement till I could recover my breath, and then I danced and cried out against the falseness of the world; and the boatmen derided me till they fell down. The chief wonder of the matter, setting aside the marvelous coldness, was that there was nothing at all in my crop when I had finished my lamenting!"

The Adjutant had done his very best to describe his feelings after swallowing a seven pound lump of Wenham Lake ice, off an American ice-ship, in the days before Calcutta made her ice by machinery; but as he did not know what ice was, and as the Mugger and the Jackal knew rather less, the tale missed fire.

While the English in London and Calcutta fondly imagined they were being supplied with very special ice, the purity of which had been testified to by the likes of Sir Charles Lyell, in reality it was the people of New York, Philadelphia, Baltimore, and Washington who were most likely to find Wenham ice in their sherry cobblers or mint juleps, with no more idea where it came from than Kipling's Adjutant Bird. But even in the Boston trade, Wenham Lake never did more than make a useful addition to local ice supplies. In 1849, Nathaniel Wyeth reckoned its ice-houses would hold ten thousand tons of ice, compared with the nearly ninety thousand that could be stored on the shores of Fresh Pond. Neither Wyeth nor Frederic Tudor left any record of what they made of the extraordinary Wenham Lake episode. The diaries Frederic had kept since 1805 end in 1838. Had he continued them, there might well have been entries vilifying the "interlopers," as he liked to call his rivals, with his own brand of "concentrated venom."

By the time the Wenham trade with England was petering out in the early 1850s, Frederic was, anyway, truly tired of the whole ice business, and began to look in earnest for someone to take over his operations. He was now in his seventies, a dapper little man with white hair and beard who was revered not only for founding the ice trade, but for the work he had carried out on his estate at Nahant. On August 4, 1852, almost forty-seven years to the day since his first icehouse diary entry, he wrote to the merchants Weld & Minot:

> I have for above a year past been considering that it is time for me to make arrangements for infusing into my business of Ice some new strength; by engaging in it some younger men. It is becoming something of a wild beast, in its strength of growth & requiring far more care & good management than I have either the will or the ability to give it.

Remarkably, this "wild beast" of an industry, which was now established throughout the eastern seaboard, from Baltimore northward, and was growing as fast as, or maybe faster than, any branch of commerce in the United States, did not figure in any official statistics. Since it could be classified as neither mining nor farming, it was not subject to any taxes that would have given federal or state governments an interest in it. Yet it had become a distinctive and important aspect of the American way of life, and in his last years, Frederic at least had the satisfaction of some attention from newspapers and magazines that began to piece together the history of this most unusual business.

Though he was no longer the leading merchant in the business, he was crowned "the Boston Ice King," purveyor of natural refrigeration to the tropics, benefactor of mankind—and, more often than not, regarded as the proprietor of that magical New England ice mine, Wenham Lake.

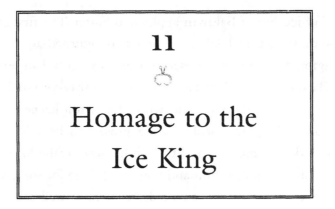

11

Homage to the Ice King

The jewel in the crown of the Boston Ice King was the Calcutta trade. Frederic reckoned that his profits over twenty years, from the time the first cargo was sent to Calcutta in 1833, amounted to $220,000. Although he also sold ice in Bombay and Madras, he had a monopoly in Calcutta, and that is where he made his real money. By winning the exclusive right to sell ice there, he fulfilled his youthful dream of becoming "inevitably and unavoidably" rich: the British community in Calcutta played a big part in wiping out his coffee debt.

The icehouse in Calcutta, built with subscription funds on land donated by the Governor-General, was a strange, domed structure that had to be enlarged several times as the demand for ice rose.* Here Frederic's agent would supervise sales not

---

*The Calcutta Ice House was demolished in the 1880s, although the Madras Ice House still exists.

only of ice, but of Baldwin apples and butter. The first agent, Marcus Bacon, had fallen ill and had returned to Boston, bringing with him as a present for his boss an Indian servant. In Bacon's place, Frederic sent out a thirty-year-old man named Caleb Ladd, who had worked as a toll keeper on the Boston to Brighton bridge. Ladd proved to be a loyal and hardworking employee, and though he never really liked Calcutta, his wife joined him and they lived there for some years. He sent regular reports to Frederic of how well sales were going:

> As for apples send me none but the very Best for one Good one is worth a dozen small Crabed [sic] ones here, and send me nothing but the Best of all Kinds of artickles for Good articles will sell for Good Profit when a cheap one will not sell at all . . . the Gentry here do not care what the price it is if they only Get the Best of every thing.

Later he wrote: "I think I shall have a small room fitted up for the retail of apples in good stile . . . the Gentry here stand all for looks and we are rite on the strand where all the first cut pass when they go out to ride and that is twice a day regular." The sale of fruit, chiefly apples, continued into the 1850s, but it did not bring in as good a profit as the ice, and Frederic finally decided it was not worth sending.

Supervised by Ladd, daily sales from the icehouse were steady. Some refrigerators were imported, but there were no deliveries of ice, as there were in America and London. A servant would be sent down with a blanket to bring home a block of ice that would last the day.

The British in Calcutta were Frederic's very best customers, conforming exactly to the image he had of a beleaguered community in the tropics thirsting for ice. In his *An Anglo-Indian Domestic Sketch* (1849), which was compiled from letters he sent back to his mother in England, the artist Colesworthy Grant wrote:

> I cannot in this place omit noticing an illustration—called to mind by that all en-grossing verb to cool—of the very singular wants which the climate and habits of a country may induce upon its inhabitants. The services of two ships—of 5 or 600 tons burthen—are retained by an American speculator for no other purpose than that of supplying the people of Calcutta with common ice—and the people of Calcutta—that is the richer portion of them—not only receive it with joy, but have built a house, of a very peculiar construction, for its reception and preservation, from where the public obtain their daily supplies at the rate of three annas per seer. With those, therefore, who avail themselves of the ice—saltpetre, patent refrigerators and all foreign contrivances are discarded for the more simple and efficacious material of nature's own preparing—by aid of which, wine, beer or drinking water, can be reduced from a state positively tepid, to a degree nearly that of zero—I will not talk of nectar or of Elysium, but I will say that if there be luxury here—

The text breaks off for a little sketch of jagged icebergs in which is written: "It is this—It is this."

In the publication *The Englishman*, which took great interest in American ice supplies from the time of the first delivery, a piece of doggerel appeared from a writer signing himself "Corn Cob":

Now kus kus tatties fail to cool
And punkah breeze defying
The mercury marks 95
And we are almost frying.

Still some relief we may enjoy
For with our "dall" and rice, Sir,
Liquids become a luxury
From Yankee Tudor's ice, sir.

This blessing answers very well
For sundry other uses
One, as a friend to you I'll tell
To Comfort it reduces.

Send for a spon [cloth] (choose a light brown)
At Bathgate's you can get it
Make a large wig to fit your crown
And with Ice *water wet it.*

Ice was also regarded as a palliative for those suffering from fevers or stomach disorders. Colesworthy Grant wrote to his mother:

> Not alone, however, as an article of luxury is the ice valued: it has been of great service used medicinally, particularly as a local application in cases of fever, so common in this country. I but lately met with a gentleman who attributed his recovery from sickness and excessive debility to having subsisted on small lumps of ice, which he swallowed, in place of every kind of warm dilutent.

It was a matter of great concern whenever the American ice failed to arrive because a ship had been delayed. The resident

Montague Massey recalled in his *Recollections of Calcutta* (1918):

> ... it occasionally happened that the vessels bringing the ice, owing to contrary winds or some other cause, were delayed, and then the stock ran low and we were put on short commons; if as in some cases the delay became very protracted the quantity allowed to each individual was gradually reduced to one seer per diem, and if any one wanted more he had to produce a doctor's certificate because it was of course imperatively necessary that sufficient should be kept in reserve for the use of the various hospitals. When the long-delayed vessel's arrival was telegraphed from Saugor [sic], great was the rejoicing of the inhabitants.

Saugar Island was at the mouth of the Hooghly River, which meant that the ice would arrive within a few days.

Surprisingly few ships were lost in the Indian ice trade— there is no record of how many—but any news of a cargo going down caused panic. In June 1837, Emily Eden, sister of the Governor-General Lord Auckland, wrote in a letter home from Calcutta:

> We are all in a horrid way about the ice, which oozed out yesterday; and no signs of an American ship; and the water we drink would make very good tea as far as warmth goes, but the Bishop had persuaded the ice managers to give him the last little scrapings of ice on the plea of our dining there.

The following month she wrote:

We had only a small dinner yesterday, for a wonder but we are very forward in our lessons, and then in this absence of ice, great dinners are so bad. Everything flops about in the dishes, and the wine and water is so hot, and a shocking thing is that a great ship was seen bottom up-wards at the mouth of the river, supposed to be an American, and consequently the ice-ship.

In an 1860s edition of his *Anglo-Indian Domestic Sketches,* Colesworthy Grant wrote:

The stoppage of the Bank of Bengal here could hardly exceed the excitement of a failure, during our hot weather, of the Ice!—and the arrival of our English mail is not more anxiously expected than that of an American Iceship, when supplies run low.

A few years after the Calcutta trade was established, Frederic's ships began calling first at Bombay, then Madras, off-loading some of their ice in each port. Landing ice in Madras was especially difficult as there was no harbor. Captain Andrew Curtis, whose ship the *Eastern Star* carried ice, Baldwin apples, and timber to Madras in the 1860s, recalled:

There is always a heavy surf on the beach and the boatmen are very skilled scarcely wetting their cargoes. The boats are large and sewed together no nails or spikes being used and capable of carrying from six to ten tons. When we began to discharge our cargo one of these native boats would come alongside and receive her load and pull ashore and through the surf landing her on the beach, where the natives would take a cake of ice in a hand-barrow and carry it a couple of hundred yards up the beach of hot white sand to the icehouse, and then up a stairway on the outside to the top, where it would be lowered into the ice-well. If the ice was wet by salt water in coming through the surf it was spoiled except for immediate sale as the water went right through it, but this rarely happened.

If there was a delay in delivery, it was the British in Bombay, the first port of call, who would be the first to learn of it. It appears that they came to regard the consignments of New England lake ice as a kind of right rather than an extraordinary accomplishment, and they were indignant when supplies ran out. In July 1850, the Bombay *Telegraph and Courier* reported:

> We are without ice! The supply is used up. The little chilly building between the Supreme Court and the Scotch Kirk is denuded of its treasures. Dirty water and sawdust is all it contains . . . If there were any such thing as public spirit in Bombay we might hope for the adoption of measures to preserve us from the recurrence of the present evil . . . There is now an interregnum: King Tudor has laid down his ice-sceptre . . . There should therefore be an agitation throughout the city . . . against the abominably sudden and inexplicable cutting off of our supply of ice.

Frederic's Bombay agent was unsympathetic. He told the newspaper that the California gold rush had led to the commandeering of so many Boston ships that it was hard to find a vessel to carry the ice. The shortage was also to some extent the fault of the British themselves, for they should have built a bigger icehouse in Bombay so that larger consignments could be delivered. However, such fallings out between the Ice King and his subjects were rare: Frederic was a heroic figure in British India, though he never visited the country, and in 1833, at the very outset of the trade, had been denied Lord Bentinck's trophy, which was rightfully his.

In Boston, it was the success of the India trade that made Frederic's reputation. He could claim that the cargoes of ice had revived the East India trade, which was failing for lack of any local commodity to export. Once the trade was reestablished, it enabled an exchange of American ice for Indian jute, the raw material for New England's mills that turned out coarse fabrics, sacks, and rope. Above all, it furthered the reputation of New England merchants as ingenious and benevolent entrepreneurs.

The first widespread recognition of the success of the ice trade came at the time of the California gold rush, which began in 1849. Gold was in everybody's mind and on everybody's lips. However, by the mid-1850s, the rapid rise of the ice industry began to attract the attention of commercial publications, and invited comparison with the gold rush. An early evaluation of the achievements and value of the ice industry was made in the August 1855 edition of *Hunt's Merchant's Magazine and Commercial Review.* The anonymous author of the piece, entitled "Ice: and the ice trade," credited Frederic Tudor with being the first to conceive of the idea that ice was salable:

> Formerly nothing was made of the ice crop of this country. The gold in these hidden mines upon our lakes was the same, but for centuries it was undiscovered wealth like that in California . . . As for the domestic use of the excellent ice which several of our northern States always afforded, in such vast quantities as to have supplied the wants of the world, it

was not thought of. And the idea of exporting to those countries and islands where nature never formed it, was not the subject of an idle dream. All this is quite a modern invention.

Frederic himself provided much of the background for the article. He must have been gratified that notice was being taken of his creation of a business out of a previously valueless resource, which was in abundant supply, at a time when a hundred thousand people had invaded California to scramble for a mineral that was valued for its rarity rather than its usefulness.

Frederic was now a grand old man with white hair and beard who spent more and more of his time out on his Nahant estate. The island had become very fashionable, and he was its great benefactor, funding the building of a causeway out from the mainland and supporting the building of a church. He managed to offend the sensibilities of Henry David Thoreau once again by erecting a fence to protect his sapling fruit trees: the writer thought this a blot on the landscape of Nahant. But otherwise he was a hero on the island, and was the subject of an unctuous address by a Boston diplomat, Edward Everett, which *Hunt's Merchant's Magazine* chose to report at length as a tribute to the inventor of the ice trade, which gave "warmth to a very cold subject":

> The gold expended by this gentleman at Nahant whether it is little or much, was originally derived not from California but from the ice of our own Fresh Pond . . . The sparkling surface of our beautiful ponds, restored by the kindly hand of nature as often as it is removed, has yielded, and will continue to yield, ages after the wet diggings and the dry diggings of the Sacramento and Feather Rivers are

exhausted, a perpetual reward to the industry bestowed upon them. The sallow genius of the mine creates but once; when rifled by man the glittering prize is gone forever. Not so with our pure crystal lakes . . .

This is a branch of the Middlesex [County] industry we have a right to be proud of. I do not think we have yet done justice to it; and I look upon Mr. Tudor, the first person who took up the business on a large scale, as a great public benefactor. He has carried comfort, in its most inoffensive and salutary form, not only to the dairies and tables of our own community, but to those of other regions, throughout the tropics, to the farthest East . . .

By way of illustration of the worldwide appreciation of Frederic's benevolence, Everett related an anecdote from his time in London. At a reception he had met a wealthy, turbaned "Hindoo," who thanked him profusely for the benefits Americans had conferred on his countrymen:

I did not at first know what he referred to; I thought he might have in view the mission schools, knowing, as I did, that he himself had done a great deal for education. He immediately said that he referred to the cargoes of ice sent from America to India; conducing not only to comfort, but health; adding that numerous lives were saved every year by applying lumps of American ice to the head of the patient in cases of high fever. He asked me if I knew from what part of America it came. It gave me great pleasure to tell him that I lived, when at home, within a short distance of the spot from which it was brought . . .

I must say I almost envied Mr. Tudor the honest satisfaction which he could not but feel in reflecting that he had been able to stretch out an arm of benevolence from the other side of the globe, by which he was every year raising up his fellows from the verge of the grave. How few of all foreigners who have entered India, from the time of Sesostris to Alexander the Great to the present time, can say as much!

In the absence of official figures on the ice industry, *Hunt's Merchant's Magazine* did its best to provide readers with the national picture at the end of 1855. Boston's preeminence in the export trade is noted, with 110,000 tons of ice going to southern cities and 48,422 tons to the East and West Indies and other foreign ports. The grand total of 156,540 tons for the previous year, 1854, included exports to Cuba, Peru, and the West Indies. Exports to England, however, had slumped:

> Of the whole of last year's exports, only 895 tons were sent to Great Britain, and that was landed at Liverpool. Years ago we were accustomed to hear how delighted the queen of England was with our Newham Lake ice. The mother-land now ships a portion of its ice from Norway, which is believed to be the only nation that exports ice, save the United States.

Wenham Lake in this report mistakenly becomes "Newham Lake," which gives some idea of how restricted its fame was in America itself, compared to Britain and India. Much better known on the eastern seaboard, and especially in New York, was Rockland Lake. According to the magazine, 120,000 tons of ice were cut from it each year, a substantial part of 285,000 tons then required to supply New York. There were huge ice stores in the city, the largest holding 113,000 tons and belonging to the Knickerbocker Ice Company. It was quite clear that by the 1850s the largest market for ice by far was America itself: "The principal towns on the Hudson lay up for home consumption about as follows:—Newburg 4,000 tons; Poughkeepsie 6,000; Hudson 4,000; Albany 20,000; Troy 10,000. Such is a general estimate furnished by a friend in New York, who is actively engaged in the business."

The magazine published a letter from Joseph Savage, an ice dealer in Syracuse, New York, to illustrate the rapid growth of the business:

> I began to supply families in 1844. The next year I supplied fifty families. In 1846 I filled an out-building with ice, and this continued until the trade became systematized. There are now very few instances of individuals putting up their own ice. This is now the practice of only two of our principal hotels, and they do this more for convenience than profit . . . The number of families who now take ice regularly is, I think, from 500 to 600 besides saloons, hotels, butchers etc. . . . We get our ice from the Onondaga Lake, a sheet of water from four or five miles long, by from one-half to two miles broad . . . The mode of cutting ice here is precisely the same as at Cambridge or Rockland. Our houses for storing are built in the same manner, and all above ground, though of less capacity.

Hunt's noted that the markets for ice in Cincinnati and Chicago had outgrown supplies from local lakes, so that shipments were now coming in from a wide area, including the Great Lakes and the rivers running into them. Other cities besides Boston were supplying southern cities:

> In Peru, Illinois, a large quantity of ice is cut, which finds a market in the towns on the Lower Mississippi River. It is

taken down the river in flat boats, and it is a curious fact that these boats are left in the autumn in the Illinois River to freeze up. When the ice is of sufficient thickness in the river it is cut and placed in the boats, that properly protected afford the only ice-houses needed. In the spring, when the ice breaks up in the river, the boats, freighted with the frozen element, are ready to float to the markets of the far South.

Philadelphia, Baltimore, and Washington cut their own ice when the winters were cold enough, but had come to rely on Boston when their harvest failed. The quality of Boston ice was also valued for its own sake: "In the best seasons they look to Boston for their best and thickest ice, such as is used in the first-class hotels; and in un-favorable seasons (say one third of the whole) the greatest portion of their supply of ice is furnished from more northern lakes."

The biggest market for Boston ice was still in the Deep South, but it was the trade between the northern states and the big cities—New York in particular—that would dominate the last and most dramatic era of the frozen-water trade. With 520 ships of all kinds engaged in the Boston ice trade in 1855, ice made up the port's largest tonnage of cargoes, though not the greatest value. *Hunt's* estimated that over America as a whole there was six to seven million dollars invested in the frozen-water trade, and that it employed between eight and ten thousand men: "From what has been said, it is clear that the ice trade is no mean one. Though it has advanced quietly, and has as yet scarcely made any figure in the literature of commerce, it is destined to be a very large business in this country."

As ice was God's gift to man, the magazine lamented the amount that was annually wasted, left to melt on lakes and rivers. While millions around the world craved the cooling and medicinal properties of ice, in America most of the "silver harvest" was left untouched. Despite the huge demand for ice and the struggle each year to harvest enough of it from lakes and rivers, the magazine makes no mention at all of the possibility of the manufacture of ice on an industrial scale. The way forward was simply to extend the harvesting of each winter's endlessly renewable supply of frozen water.

In December 1855, *De Bow's Review,* published in Washington and New Orleans, ran an account of the growth of the ice trade, which it described as "a thoroughly worthy notion of a solid man of that City of Notions." Most of the magazine's facts and figures were taken from *Hunt's;* what was new was the account it gave of the degree to which ice had become regarded as a necessity of life:

> Ice is an American institution—the use of it an American luxury—the abuse of it an American failing. As in the matter of luxuries, as in government, we are democratic and popular, the great mass of the people moving, living and having a being in America, can and do enjoy these creature comforts of existence daily, which are, in European nations, the Sabbath wonder of the humbler domestic circles . . . The use of ice is esteemed a rare blessing there, and like all good things beyond the water, is adopted by the aristocracies.
>
> Dietetically, the poorer, and even middle classes know nothing of ice. It is confined to the cellars of the rich and the cooling pantries of first class confectioners.

It was not just a question of climate, according to *De Bow's Review*—European countries were often as hot as New York in summer. In America, everyone had ice if they wanted it, in whichever region they lived:

> In workshops, composing rooms, counting houses, workmen, printers, clerks club have their daily supply of ice. Every office, nook or cranny, illuminated by a human face, is also cooled by the presence of his crystal friend . . . It is as good as oil to the wheel. It sets the whole human machinery in pleasant action, turns the wheels of commerce, and propels the energetic business engine. In every house almost there is a vein of ice, beginning with the blocks in the cellar and going through the refrigerators and filters on every story to the attic . . . We use it seven or eight months of the year—all the year in the south; and even in New York there are numbers of families who ice their Croton [drinking water from Lake Croton, to the north of the city] throughout the winter. In this latter particular, and in the too free and careless use of it in the hottest days of summer, the abuse of the luxury consists. It is considered by physicians as a tonic; but an excess, as in the use of intoxicating liquors, will, in all probability produce diarrhea.

The magazine assumed that most of its readers would have little idea what effort went into the production of "the little piece of ice" they popped into their glasses, and retold the Tudor story, which was by now becoming a familiar tale of triumph over adversity:

> For twenty years, considerable disappointment, with various success, attended his efforts, but ultimately his persistency and activity furnished the southern States and the

West Indies with the frozen delicacy and a lucrative business opened up.

This all came from the horse's mouth—there is no mention at all of Nathaniel Wyeth and his vital contribution to the trade. Nor had there been in *Hunt's Merchant's Magazine,* except the comment that N. J. Wyeth had "joined" Tudor in the business. Yet the scene of ice cutting that *Hunt's* described would not have been possible without Wyeth's inventions:

> One of the most attractive drives in good sleighing from Boston and neighborhood is to Fresh Pond, to witness the process of securing a precious harvest. The pond is pleasantly nestled among hills of a moderate height. Of a pleasant afternoon on a winter's day, hundreds of sleighs may be found there filled with well-dressed persons of both sexes, full of life, and on the que vive to witness the wonderful operations before them. If they are paying their first winter visit, the sights before them are strange indeed—the silvery pond glaring under the oblique rays of the sun—the dark blue waters from which the ice has already been removed—the curious and huge buildings that fringe its shores—the hundreds of laborers with scores of horses that almost darken the pond, each aiming at usefulness according to their several ability—the curious mode of removing the snow and ice—of working and cutting the marketable solid—the floating it through narrow artificial canals—and, above all, the storing of it by the wonderful power of steam—all these things quite fill the crowds of spectators with admiration, and they feel paid if they have performed a journey of thirty miles merely to witness them.

Wyeth's last significant technological improvement had been to power the conveyors with steam engines that carried the ice into the icehouse.

A year after this description of Fresh Pond harvesting was published, Wyeth died at the age of fifty-four. In August 1856, the *Boston Transcript* wrote: "It is not perhaps too much to say that there is not a single tool or machine of real value now employed in the ice harvesting, which was not originally invented by Mr. Wyeth. They all look to Fresh Pond as the place of their origin."

Wyeth always shunned publicity, and had none of Frederic Tudor's desire for fame. Later in the century, he was feted not as the great inventor of the ice industry, but as a pioneer who had laid the foundations for the wresting of Oregon from the British. During the conflict that would lead to the establishment of Oregon as the thirty-third American state in 1859, Fort Hall, which Wyeth had built, proved crucial. The fact that he had sold it to the British, in the form of the Hudson's Bay Company, to fund his ice business appears to have been forgotten, and he was awarded posthumous fame as an American patriot, when in reality he had gone to Oregon simply to make money, a venture that was an abject failure.

Frederic was now the lone survivor from the early days of the ice industry, and in January 1857, he made his last grand statement in a special report to the Boston Board of Trade. The four short pages glow with pride in what he had created. In the previous year, a total of 363 cargoes of ice, amounting to 146,000 tons, had been shipped from Boston around the world.

To Calcutta, Bombay, and Madras in India were added many places in the West Indies, as well as Manila, Singapore, Canton, and Australia. And the trade in Boston itself had grown very rapidly: "There are 93 wagons and about 150 horses employed in distributing ice in Boston and vicinity; 60,000 tons are thus retailed, supplying 18,000 families, hotels, stores and factories." Fishermen kept their catches fresh in ice; passenger steamers were using it to preserve food, and had thus gotten rid of the inconvenience of keeping livestock aboard. In short, daily life was rapidly being transformed; and this was only the beginning: "The ice trade was born here in Boston, and has been growing and extending itself, with no successful competition, for more than half a century, as has been stated above and there is reason to think that it is yet in its infancy."

Frederic was right about the ice industry being in its infancy: the quantity harvested in America rose every year until the first decade of the twentieth century, and would be measured not in thousands but in millions of tons. But Boston lost its preeminence when much richer ice fields were opened up to the north and in the Midwest from the 1860s onward. The challenge from the artificial manufacture of ice was negligible, though the first working models, which were the forerunners of modern refrigerators, came on the market at about the time Frederic was writing his triumphant report for the Boston Board of Trade.

For a number of years, cargoes of ice had been sent to the town of Apalachicola, in Florida, where it was in demand in hospitals to treat those suffering from malaria and yellow fever.

It was not until the start of the twentieth century that mosquitoes were identified as the carriers of both these diseases—the
word "malaria" means simply "bad air," and "yellow" fever
described the jaundiced complexion of those who caught the
disease. A physician working in the naval hospital in
Apalachicola in the 1840s, Dr. John Gorrie, believed that ice-
cooled air was a valuable curative for his patients, but was
unhappy with the intermittent supply of natural ice. He had
noted that "nature would terminate the fevers by changing the
seasons," by which he meant that both malaria and yellow fever
struck in the summer rather than the winter. He had an idea
that the swamplands of Florida had something to do with out-
breaks of malaria and yellow fever, but thought it was the hot air
that was to blame. His first attempt to cool down the hospital
wards involved suspending blocks of ice high in the air and
directing a current of air from a chimney over them.

Others before Dr. Gorrie had worked out in principle, and
occasionally in practice, how to create artificial cold by com-
pressing air or other gases and then releasing the pressure, so that
the energy used up in their expansion drew heat from water that
was in contact with the gas container. Compression required
some source of power: an American, Jacob Perkins, who lived in
London in the 1830s, had built a refrigerator of this kind using
the tidal flow of the River Thames to drive it. Dr. Gorrie constructed a strange-looking contraption—there is a model of it
in the Gorrie Museum in Apalachicola—which could be powered by water, wind sails, horses, or steam. Whereas later and
more successful refrigerators used ether or ammonia as the gas

that was compressed and then allowed to expand, Gorrie's used just air. He explained his invention in a series of articles in the Apalachicola *Commercial Advertiser* in 1844:

> If the air were highly compressed, it would heat up by the energy of compression. If this compressed air were run through metal pipes cooled with water, and if this air cooled to the water temperature was expanded down to atmospheric pressure again, very low temperature could be obtained, even low enough to freeze water in pans in a refrigerator box.

After making a wood-and-metal prototype, Gorrie went to an ironworks in Cincinnati, Ohio, to get a more substantial model built. He was awarded a British patent in 1850 and a United States patent the following year. Armed with these, he went to New Orleans with the idea of turning his invention into a going commercial concern. But nobody was interested. A look at the Gorrie refrigerator, and a comparison of the few ice blocks it could produce with a cargo of lake ice from Boston, shows why. New Orleans was consuming thousands of tons of ice, and Gorrie's invention would have contributed an insignificant amount. It was also less reliable in its operation than the well-run frozen-water trade that he hoped to replace. Gorrie died in 1855 without selling a single machine, his contribution to refrigeration in the United States the same as the temperature he created artificially—zero.

In 1857, the same year as Frederic's Boston Board of Trade report, Alexander Catlin Twining published a booklet called *The Manufacture of Ice on a Commercial Scale*. Twining, a mathematician and engineer from New York, was a professor at Middlebury College in Vermont. He became interested in refrigeration, and experimented using ether rather than air. Like Gorrie, he had a machine built. He chose Cleveland, Ohio, to promote his invention, but was unable to compete with the natural-ice harvesters. By 1860, the Frenchman Ferdinand Carré had patented in the United States the most efficient refrigerator yet developed, using ammonia as the refrigerant gas. It was his more sophisticated apparatus that was the first to go into commercial production in the American south, though it did so without making any inroads in the natural-ice trade.

Quite oblivious to these developments, in 1859, Frederic Tudor had embarked on a new venture to amuse the people of Boston. He had been buying land on Nahant, and now owned ten acres of coast that looked north toward the fishing village of Marblehead. On Frederic's land was a freshwater spring, which was the inspiration for him to create an amusement park he named Maolis. In his way a devout man, Frederic was familiar with the Bible, and the spring on Nahant reminded him of the pool in Jerusalem named Siloam, where Jesus had cured a man of blindness. "Maolis" is "Siloam" backward, and what Frederic called the "Pool of Maolis" was a feature of his pleasure garden. Even in the last years of his life—he was now seventy-five— Frederic sought to profit from providing others with what he regarded as pleasure. His little park was full of attractions. There was, of course, an ice cream pavilion, as well as a place where people could cook their own picnic food, provided they bought from Frederic the wood needed to fire the stoves. A "Moses Rock" was devised that would spout water when tapped with a stick, and there was a "Witch House" to frighten the children. There was a teahouse and a dance hall, a grotto decorated entirely with shells, and, to complete the fairground atmosphere, a huge swing suspended on fifty-foot poles, a bowling alley, a rifle range, and a Punch and Judy show. There were two entrances, one for visitors on foot and another for those in carriages. Adults paid five cents and children three, and all were encouraged to arrive with their pockets full of cash to spend on the various amusements. This extraordinary project, which upset a few Nahant residents as it attracted some of the lower orders from Boston, was the last of Frederic's long life. He did not make much money from it, and he did not need to. He was just enjoying himself.

Effie had given birth to their fifth child, Eleanor, in 1850, and their sixth and last, a boy named Henry, was born with a mental disability in 1854, when Frederic was seventy-one years old and Effie forty-one. Early in 1864, Frederic's health began to fail, and he died on Saturday, February 6, at the age of eighty. A few months later, his brother-in-law Robert Gardiner, whom he had seen occasionally since their falling out in 1839, also died. Not long after that, his younger brother, Harry, who had helped set up the New Orleans trade, also died.

In 1860, Frederic had created the Tudor Ice Company, which was run by a member of the Minot family and specialized in the export trade to Havana, India, and the southern ports. Before Frederic died, he had a legal wrangle with his wife over her inheritance, and in the end Effie got the business. She changed her Christian name to Fenno, her maiden name. After Frederic's death, she read his diaries going back to the time they were married, and peppered them with angry annotations. The most startling of these is on an entry from February 1834, the month after their wedding:

> It could hardly be expected that a honeymoon would last after the wife had discovered that the marriage privileges were shared with a woman who had lived with him with occasional interruptions since 1824. That in my youth and helplessness I should have felt compelled to a complicity in what the laws recognise as crimes my children must excuse as best they may.

We do not know who this other woman was. Frederic's boarding-house keeper in Boston? Someone out at Nahant?

Frederic was evidently not a hero as far as his widow was concerned, but he had won the hearts of people from Nahant to Calcutta. This short epitaph was published in the *Annals of Lynn,* the district that included Nahant:

> He was a man of great decision of character, promptness in action, and impatience of interference with his plans. Towards strangers he manifested great courtesy and did much to render their visits to Nahant agreeable. The inhabitants, at their annual town meeting 12 March 1864 unanimously adopted resolutions expressive of their sense of loss and appreciation of his worth and generosity.

The Boston Ice King was dead, but the industry he had fashioned through sheer determination was alive and growing fast.

12

After Tudor

In his last years, Frederic Tudor had had the satisfaction of seeing his youthful dream of making a fortune from frozen water fulfilled. His was a remarkable story, and the scale and enterprise of the ice trade by the 1860s was impressive. But North America's dependence on natural-lake and natural-river ice had barely begun. While one inventor after another claimed he could manufacture ice that was cheaper and of better quality than that harvested each winter, their inventions made practically no impact on refrigeration at all until forty years after Frederic's death.

Winter ice was so abundant in the northern United States, and the techniques of cutting, storing, and shipping it so efficient, that it continued to supply the annual requirements of the whole nation even as the demand rose year by year. The icehouses, the steam elevators, and the great activity of men and horses that had so impressed *Hunt's Merchant's Magazine* at Fresh Pond in 1855 were by the 1880s being repeated on a larger scale in an industry that thrived in Maine, Wisconsin, and Pennsylvania, and could be found wherever there was a demand for ice and a convenient source of it. Fleets of ships continued to carry the ice in the East Coast trade, while the railroads that now crisscrossed the United States had opened up the interior to the distribution of ice over hundreds and even thousands of miles.

The taste for iced drinks and ice cream, and the increasing ownership of domestic refrigerators refreshed daily in the summer by the ice delivery men, made for a huge demand among the general population, with New York by far the largest market. But by the 1880s, the biggest consumers of natural ice were the brewing and fresh-food industries. Americans had developed a taste for German lager beer, which can only be brewed successfully at low temperatures. Without refrigeration, lager could be brewed only in the winter. Ice enabled the brewers to work the year round, making for a rapid expansion of the industry. As the beer was drunk cold, that increased the demand for ice supplies in hotels and homes. Milwaukee, on the western shores of Lake Michigan, had a substantial German population and became (as it remains) the center of lager-beer manufacture, with an assured supply of winter ice from the Milwaukee River and the lakes of Wisconsin.

On the southern tip of Lake Michigan, Chicago grew into the great meat-packing center, where drovers arrived with huge herds of cattle for slaughter. To sell meat outside the local market, refrigeration was essential, and two companies, Swift and

Armour, arose that specialized in the manufacture and running of wagons cooled with natural ice. Both companies owned thousands of refrigerated railroad cars that had to be continuously replenished with ice. This was stored at railroad junctions next to the coal and water needed for the steam engines, and Armour's yellow sheds became a familiar feature of the Midwest and along the chief routes to New York, New Orleans, and California. These specialist shippers became ice harvesters in their own right, buying up sections of lakeshore and building gigantic icehouses, some of which had a capacity of 250,000 tons. The refrigerated wagons carried not only meat from Chicago, but South American bananas that were shipped to New Orleans and carried from there on the Illinois Central railroad up to Chicago. Armour also carried fruit and vegetables from the West Coast to the Midwest, replenishing the ice in its wagons from depots in the high Sierra Nevada mountains. Although some artificial refrigeration systems were operating by this time, they were steam driven, and not suitable for the chilling of railway wagons. Natural ice, in any case, was cheap.

The huge ice industry that grew up around Chicago and Milwaukee was only one of the spectacular developments in the trade that came after Tudor. Another, which he did not foresee, was the rise of ice harvesting in Maine, where his brother-in-law Robert Gardiner had had his estate. As far as Tudor and Nathaniel Wyeth had been concerned, the tidal Kennebec River was useful for emergency supplies when Massachusetts ice was in short supply. But for reasons they could not have anticipated, in the 1870s the Kennebec became a much more significant source of ice than Fresh Pond. Winters were, on average, getting warmer, and the more southerly state of Massachusetts had poorer ice crops than Maine. When there was an "open winter" all the way up the eastern seaboard from Baltimore to Boston, an "ice famine" was declared, and Maine became the supplier of last resort. In fact, New York would rely on Maine ice in most years from the 1870s until the end of the First World War.

The first stimulus for the Kennebec industry was not, however, a harvest failure farther south. The American Civil War, in which the confederation of southern, slave-owning states fought and lost the right to secede from the northern states of the Union, broke out in 1861 and continued until 1865. The bloody battles that left around 600,000 dead were fought well to the south of Massachusetts and Maine, and did not interfere with the harvesting of ice. However, the important markets in the south were cut off when Abraham Lincoln declared a blockade of Confederate ports. Boston could continue to send ice to the East Indies to compensate for the loss of the New Orleans trade, and the Union armies provided a new market that could be supplied along the East Coast.

In 1860, a New York ice harvester from the Hudson, James L. Cheeseman, had shifted his operations to the village of Farmingdale, on the Kennebec River, and established a well-run business there, building large icehouses and using the most up-to-date ice-cutting and storing equipment. When the Civil War broke out, he won a contract to supply the Union army with ice at very high prices. This began the trade between Maine and the fast-growing East Coast cities of New York, Washington, Baltimore, and Philadelphia, which expanded very rapidly in the 1870s, outstripping Boston's ice trade by hundreds of thousands of tons of ice a year.

Although Boston lost its market in the southern states during the war, this was well compensated for by the growth of the India trade, still dominated by the Tudor Ice Company. Whereas in the 1850s the annual amount of ice shipped to Calcutta, Bombay, and Madras had been between 3,000 and 3,500 tons, it rose to 8,000 tons in 1863. Unable to carry cotton from the southern plantations, Boston ships were instead bringing in cargoes from India, and the increased traffic stimulated the ice trade. The Tudor Ice Company books show a profit of $377,000 between 1864 and 1866 from Calcutta alone. The trade continued to grow until 1870, when, according to British India Office reports, 17,000 tons of American ice was imported in that year alone. Not all of this would have been shipped by the Tudor Ice Company, for there were now rivals supplying the Indian market.

Throughout the 1870s, India continued to receive about 12,000 tons of American ice a year, and the Tudor Ice Company was confident enough that the trade would continue to grow to have three ships built: the *Iceking,* which bore a large figurehead of Frederic; the *Iceberg*; and the *Iceland.* These fine square-riggers were a new departure for the company, which had previously chartered ships to carry its ice. Sadly, the *Iceland* was wrecked in 1877, a year after its launch, by which time the Calcutta trade was already close to its end. The first successful manufacturer of artificial ice with a steam-driven refrigerator system opened for business in India in 1878, and was soon challenged by a rival.

Fearing that they would drive each other out of business if they competed, these two rivals, the Bengal Ice Manufacturing Company and the Crystal Ice Company, merged, and were soon able to undercut the prices of the Tudor Ice Company. By 1882, the old trade was dead.

The replacement for Tudor ice was not, however, entirely satisfactory. The following letter appeared in the Calcutta *Statesman* on May 3, 1881, when the Bengal Ice Manufacturing Company had not long been in production:

> Sir, I have looked every morning expecting to find you calling the Ice Company to task for the disgraceful manner in which they are at present catering for the wants of the public. On two or three occasions my servant has returned saying there was no ice at all; at other times when I have written a letter the same has been thrown away and the man told to go. The other evening several gentlemen went themselves but could obtain no ice.

The editor replied that the *Statesman* always got its ice (perhaps to keep it quiet), and that the company should think of getting more power, so as to be able to produce more ice. He added: "While on the subject, we may remark that the ice is not always so pure as it should be. There is sometimes a whitish sediment in the glass."

New Orleans found it hard to get any ice at all during the Civil War, but its citizens were enterprising enough to have two artificial ice-making machines designed by the Frenchman Ferdinand Carré smuggled from France through the shipping blockade. These could not replace the supplies of natural-lake ice, and what they produced was used chiefly to cool hospital wards, but it was the beginning of commercial ice manufacture in America, which was to make steady but very slow progress over the next half century.

It was only in the Gulf states of the south that artificial refrigeration was of any real significance, for they were a long way from the chief sources of natural ice, which was necessarily more expensive for them than it was farther north. Elsewhere, there was no possibility of manufactured ice meeting the rapidly growing demands of industry and the big cities: the only solution was to develop the natural-ice industry, and big companies, like prospectors drilling for oil, went in search of new sources.

For New York, Philadelphia, Washington, and Baltimore, the chief source of extra supplies was Maine, with the greatest concentration of harvesters on the Kennebec River. Because it flows north to south with a steep gradient, when the Kennebec runs into the sea at Merrymaking Bay, the rush of freshwater holds back the saltwater of the sea, and though the tides run for miles inland, the water is not brackish. Most winters in the late nineteenth century, the Kennebec, and other Maine rivers such as the Penobscot and the Sheepscot, as well as freshwater lakes, froze solid to a depth of eighteen inches or more. There was therefore an abundance of ice that could be cut and stored in icehouses on the shore to await shipment when the river ice broke up, usually in late March or early April. Then schooners would sail up the rivers and load ice directly from the shore, be towed out into the bay, and sail south to deliver their cargoes. As a return cargo, they often took coal from Philadelphia to Maine, which thus kept itself warm in winter while keeping the more southerly states cool in summer. Sea captains engaged in this trade would often say they were "ice and coaling."

The demand for Maine ice was dependent on the winter weather each year. What Maine ice harvesters hoped for was a blazing-hot summer down south, followed by a mild winter that would ruin the harvest in the other main ice-producing states. Maine's first big break came in the winter of 1869–70, when the harvest failed on the Hudson River and everywhere south of Massachusetts, while Boston too was short of ice. The few companies harvesting ice on the Kennebec River engaged in a mad scramble to cut and ship as much ice as physically possible, so as to benefit from the rising prices in New York and other cities. In a few weeks, three hundred thousand tons was cut, three times the annual average. From that time on, the state of the ice in Maine was a regular item in the newspapers of the major cities that got their supplies from farther north.

The New York ice companies that had been formed in the 1850s harvested their supplies locally from the Hudson River and inland lakes, and had little trouble satisfying demand for a decade or so. But the rising consumption of ice in the city left them vulnerable to shortages in mild winters, and they became the butt of much criticism in the *New York Times* and other newspapers, accused of deliberately limiting supply just to keep the price of ice high.

After the mild winter of 1869–70 when the New York, Washington, Philadelphia, and Baltimore companies had to pay a very high price for ice shipped down from Maine, they decided to buy up land on the banks of the Kennebec River and to build huge wooden icehouses all along it. Although the owners of the ice were now outsiders such as the Knickerbocker companies of New York and Philadelphia, the industry remained essentially a local one, and brought some prosperity to blacksmiths, carpenters, farmers, and shipping interests in the region. Ten years after the first Kennebec ice bonanza, there was another spectacular one in 1880. When in February it was realized that the ice harvest to the south had failed, while the ice was fifteen to twenty inches thick on the Kennebec and free of snow, there was once again a crazy scramble to cut as many tons as possible and ship it south. The Penobscot and Sheepscot Rivers, which had previously had a small trade, were cut by local teams of men who bought up every piece of ice-harvesting equipment they could to profit from the rising prices in the cities to the south.

If Frederic Tudor could have seen it, he would not have believed the evidence of his eyes. Everything was still done exactly as it had been in his day: the surface of the ice was scraped clean, it was marked out and plowed by teams of horses, floated to the conveyor belts at the icehouse, and then loaded onto schooners in its insulation of sawdust. Everybody who could turned their hand to the harvest. Sawdust was in high demand, and derelict sawmills were pillaged for shavings that had been left as worthless years before, but could now be sold to the shippers. Marsh hay, which was also used for insulation, doubled in price from $5 to $10 a ton. It was estimated that on just four miles of the frozen Kennebec River in the winter of 1879–80 there was an army of 4,000 men and 350 horses working day and night. When the icehouses were full to capacity, stacks were made on the bank. By the time the ice was all in, just under 1 million tons had been taken from the Kennebec, 150,000 from the Penobscot, and 110,000 from the Sheepscot. With ice from a few other sources, this made a grand total of 1.3 million tons gathered in a month or so. An estimated six hundred thousand dollars was paid to the workforce who harvested and loaded the ice; and the cost of shipping was one million dollars, but it made a good profit.

It was perhaps this extraordinary "ice rush" that first prompted the United States Census to take a look at the industry. A report was commissioned in 1880, and was published in June 1883 as an appendix to the 1880 national census. It was written by Special Agent Henry Hall. In the absence of any official figures, Hall had made extensive inquiries in the ice business, and produced the best estimates he could for production and consumption throughout the United States. He reckoned that during what he called "the great excitement" in Maine in 1880, of the 1.3 million tons of ice cut, nearly a million was shipped south in two thousand cargoes carried by 1,735 vessels, mostly schooners. At the end of the harvest, there were, on the Kennebec River, thirty-six ice companies whose fifty-three icehouses had a holding capacity of over a million tons. Hall concluded: "On the short stretch of river from Bath to Hallowell there is now more capital concentrated in the cutting and storage of ice than in any other locality of equal extent in the world."

By comparison, Hall found that the manufacture of artificial ice was negligible. It was only in the Gulf states, which were a long way from the sources of natural ice, that a significant amount was produced. Hall gives a detailed account of the kind of steam-driven ice plant used by the Louisiana Ice Company in New Orleans. The system was the same as that patented by Ferdinand Carré in 1860, using vaporized ammonia that was heated up and then cooled in a steam-driven apparatus. Carré had found a way of recycling the ammonia gas in the system, which greatly cut the costs of manufacturing ice: earlier models needed to be "refueled" continuously. Each of the Louisiana Ice Company's machines produced about eighteen to nineteen tons of ice a day, giving the company a total annual output of about forty-five thousand. By the 1880s, there were many similar machines in operation in the inland towns of the southern Gulf states, though most of them produced smaller quantities of ice than the Louisiana Ice Company, and their contribution to America's annual ice production was very small. They had only local importance in places where natural ice had to be imported at very high prices. At this time, there were about forty different styles of ice machine in operation around the world, and a hundred had been patented in Washington. Hall commented: "Not over half a dozen, however, are in this country considered of much practical value."

Artificial-ice manufacturers faced a number of difficulties. Because of the high pressures required to expand gases, there were often leaks from the joints of the crudely made machines. Oil could get onto the ice and contaminate it, and there was also a danger of explosions—quite a few did blow up in the early years. On the Kennebec River, any news of an artificial-ice disaster was greeted with glee. The Bath, Maine, *Daily Times* reported in January 1889:

Kennebec ice men can now chuckle under their high collars and mark up several points for their natural river product. An ice machine in Chicago, which was busily trying to run out the real frost product, has just blown up, setting fire to buildings and doing $200,000 damage. A few accidents like this will discourage the general introduction of such concerns, and Maine's winter industry will continue to flourish as of old.

The single biggest challenge for the artificial-ice manufacturers was to find a way of undercutting the price of the "real frost product." Hall concluded:

> In order to carry on a successful business in artificial ice-making the product must be manufactured at a cost not to exceed $2 to $3 a ton. The chief cause of the numerous disastrous failures so far has been that the product cost anywhere from $20 to $250 a ton. One American proprietor lost $100,000 in experiments in New Orleans before success was achieved. It has been the aim of inventors in this country to make ice at from seventy-five cents to $1 a ton. Many times during the last ten years the announcement has been made that the result has been accomplished. It is doubtful if, in practice, any ice-maker in America has yet been able to produce ice so cheaply.

There was also the question of whether artificial-ice manufacturers could, with the technology they had, get anywhere near satisfying the demand for ice at any price. As the magazine *The American Ship* put it in 1880: "Ice machines would be as useful in supplying New York as a boy's squirt-gun at a fire. Running full time, one of them can make six tons per day, while the requirements of a single company in the summer season are 250 tons a day."

In the absence of official figures, Hall attempted to gather what statistics he could from various states and companies to estimate the quantities of ice harvested in the winter of 1879–80, the degree of wastage through breakage and melting, and the amount eventually sold to the public and to industry. The grand total he came up with for consumption was more than 5 million tons. New York was far and away the largest market, requiring 956,000 tons; Brooklyn, evaluated separately, used 334,500. In Chicago, the consumption was estimated at nearly 580,000 tons; in Boston, 381,600 tons; and in Philadelphia, 377,000 tons. All in all, twenty large cities with a total population of just under 6 million bought nearly 4 million tons of ice in one year. To satisfy this demand, it was estimated that between 8 and 10 million tons of ice had been harvested in the census year. Hall wrote:

> It is not the quantity that forms in any given winter, however, which is of the greatest consequence. Interest attaches only to the quantity actually harvested and stored away in ice-houses in different parts of the country. The possession of such unlimited ice resources is of great importance to the United States. It is a remarkable fact that in some localities the communities already pay out as much money for ice in the course of the year as they do for [winter] fuel.

Hall believed that there was never likely to be a shortage of ice, for he estimated that one square mile of ice a foot thick when cut would yield 700,000 tons, meaning that "any little lake" of fifteen square miles could supply the whole country. While this was true in theory, in practice there were problems with ice harvesting. Only those sources close to markets or to some convenient means of transport would ever be exploited, and these were becoming scarce in some regions. Even around Chicago and Milwaukee, a mild winter could cut back the ice crop and produce a "famine." At the same time, the sources of ice closest to the big cities were becoming contaminated with sewage from the rising populations, and in the 1880s, the first concerns were expressed about the dangers of using ice cut from rivers and lakes that were putrid in summer. Whereas along the Kennebec the settlements were not much more than villages, satellite towns in New York were growing rapidly along the Hudson River, and in the Midwest, Milwaukee and Chicago began to face serious pollution problems. Health authorities began to ban the cutting of ice close to towns.

By the end of the century, the big cities on the eastern seaboard had a well-developed source of regular and emergency supplies of ice from Maine, and cities in the Midwest began to look to the wilder regions of Wisconsin, inland from Lake Michigan. There were many freshwater lakes that had been dammed to provide waterpower for mills of various kinds, and these produced excellent crops of clear ice. The railroads had made some of these accessible for harvesting, and the ice companies of Chicago and Milwaukee began to exploit them from the 1880s onward. Just as there had been disputes over the ownership of Fresh Pond ice in the 1840s, now there were battles for the lakes of Wisconsin; and they were not always settled in a very gentlemanly fashion. Many of the ice harvesters in the last decade of the nineteenth century were newly arrived immigrants from Europe—Germans, Poles, and Hungarians who could pick up a few dollars a day in winter when work elsewhere was scarce. The ice companies of Milwaukee and Chicago employed many of these rugged young men on the winter harvest, and this sometimes gave rise to national rivalries.

The Midwest natural-ice industry was still going strong in the first years of the twentieth century, and it was here, on the Milwaukee River, that possibly the most spectacular battle between rival companies in the frozen-water trade took place. In 1900, a new enterprise was formed in Milwaukee, calling itself the Pike and North Lake Company, to take ice from two clear inland lakes at a time when the Milwaukee River was becoming seriously polluted. A well-established rival concern, the Wisconsin Lakes Ice and Cartage Company, was still cutting its ice from the river, and was not pleased at the prospect of this interloper advertising its ice as "purer"—which it most certainly would have been.

The Pike company built large icehouses conveniently close to a railroad, and it was only after they had begun cutting and storing ice that they discovered they did not own the land between the icehouses and the railroad. When they attempted to buy this land, they found that an agent had already gotten possession of it on behalf of an anonymous owner who refused to sell. Naturally, the Pike company suspected the Wisconsin company of being the mystery owner that had sabotaged their new venture, leaving them unable to shift their ice. Many of the

Wisconsin company harvesters were Polish immigrants, while the Pike company recruited Germans. The scene was set for a spectacular ice war that would rage for weeks that winter.

On January 1, 1901, the Pike company, denied the use of its harvest, advertised unseasonal "river excursions" on the Milwaukee River, which the Wisconsin company was about to cut. The trips were aboard a steam launch named the *Julius Goll* that had been fitted out as an ice breaker and heavily reinforced with boiler plate. A German band played as it set off through the river ice, smashing its way through the Wisconsin company's supplies until they were broken up and useless. Despite pitched battles between the men of the two companies, the *Julius Goll's* cruises could not be stopped. For six weeks, it continued to smash up the ice whenever it formed.

The fullest reports of the conflict were in the German-language *Milwaukee Herald,* which showed surprise when the courts declined to convict anyone after the battle was over. Very soon, many such conflicts would be resolved by the rapid consolidation of rival ice companies, which had already begun in Chicago and on the eastern seaboard. Instead of the amusing but wasteful spectacle of watching competing companies knock lumps out of each other, the public faced the grim prospect of monopoly power in the ice industry.*

---

*Following the battle between the Pike company and the Wisconsin company, there was an attempt in Wisconsin to claim that all the ice was owned by the state. Local legislation—the Overbeck Ice Bill—was enacted requiring ice-harvesting companies to pay for the right to cut ice on Wisconsin's lakes. However, the large Knickerbocker company successfully challenged this law in the state supreme court, and it was repealed in 1903.

Though the motive of those who sought to create huge ice companies that would be able to hold the public for ransom might have been simply profit, there was also a logic to amalgamation in the last years of the nineteenth century. The capital required to build and equip icehouses had become too great for smaller concerns, which were vulnerable to fluctuations in supply and demand. On the Kennebec, a typical icehouse with a spruce framework and cedar shingling for the roof and walls might be three hundred feet long and contain a number of "rooms" with separate store "dumps." The crews who worked to lay up the huge crystal blocks at the time of the harvest and to load them onto ships in the spring had become highly specialized, shifting the cakes of ice around on wooden slides as if they were engaged in a giant version of the Scottish game of curling.

The elevators that took the ice from the river were steam driven, but the work inside the icehouses was all manual. The ice came in from the top of the house and was run down wooden chutes, its speed checked by men with picks of various kinds. Stevedores supervised the stacking, which did not stop until all the layers of ice reached the ceiling. On the Kennebec, there was usually a gap of a few weeks between the end of the harvest and the opening of the river for shipping. The unloading of the icehouse began from the top. Crews had what were called "dump runs," sections of ice to be shifted using a movable wood-and-iron runway to the icehouse doors. A chiseler broke each individual block free, then a barman would lever it toward two men called "breakers," who worked on either side of the cake of ice—it helped if one was right-handed and the other left-handed. Although skilled crews could move the ice blocks with little breakage, there were always chips that had to be cleared away; this was the job of the shoveler, known on the Kennebec as a "chip Joe" or "banjo artist." Once they were set moving on the dump run, the blocks were steered onto a straight run out to the waiting ship, and lowered into the hold by a mechanism a bit like a dumbwaiter, with two cakes at a time weighing down a platform balanced by a pulley system having a box of rocks on the other end of a rope. All the wooden mechanisms in the icehouse had to be movable so they could be set in new positions as the tiers of ice were taken away.

By the 1890s, schooners, towed by steam tug to the ocean, were taking loads of up to 1,800 tons of ice at a time. Later, sailing barges, which were cheaper to run, were used to get the ice to New York and other markets to the south. The harvesting rights and icehouses were often owned by companies based in the cities where the ice was sold, who would send up representatives to check the amounts stored and shipped. But most of the workforce in Maine was local, or drawn from the lumber industry, which ceased work in midwinter. The men who came from the woods were put up in company boardinghouses or took lodgings locally. Their arrival in late December or January provided local farmers with useful income. All the ice companies operated in more or less the same way: if not enough horses could be provided locally, they shipped their own—used to deliver the ice in summer—up from New York, Baltimore, Washington, and Philadelphia.

This was big business, and someone was bound to look for a way of monopolizing the trade. On the Kennebec, the oppor-

tunity came with the greatest bonanza in the history of the
Maine ice industry in the winter of 1890–91. When the harvest
farther south failed completely, three million tons of Maine ice
was cut and loaded onto schooners. However, when the ships
arrived in New York, Philadelphia, and Baltimore, the spring
was surprisingly cool, and the demand for ice consequently
low. In his census report of 1883, Henry Hall had shown in a
series of graphs how the demand for ice varied considerably
with summer temperatures: the industry ideal was bitter winters
and boiling summers. In 1891, the demand remained low, and
many companies on the Kennebec lost money, and schooners
lay idle. This gave an ambitious young man from Maine,
Charles S. Morse, his big break. His family had been in the ice
trade for years, and owned most of the tugs that took the
schooners out to sea. When the ice trade in Maine collapsed
after this bumper harvest, Morse bought up a number of companies and formed the Consolidated Ice Company, with capital
of ten million dollars. He then moved to New York, where he
began to acquire more ice companies. By 1900, he had a virtual
monopoly in the city with his American Ice Company, valued
at sixty million dollars. Morse became known as the "New York
Ice King."

On May 6, 1900, the *New York Times* carried a six-column
article with the shocking headline "ONE HUNDRED PER
CENT RISE IN ICE—New York's Trust Limits Harvest and
Controls Distribution—American Company, However, Has a
Monopoly and Squeezes Rich and Poor Alike." The previous
year, families in Manhattan and the Bronx had paid about thirty
cents per hundred pounds of ice; now they were being asked for

sixty cents, as the price the American Ice Company was charging wholesale had risen from $5.50 a ton to $15.50. When Charles Morse was asked why prices had doubled, he blamed the "open winter" on the Hudson. It was true that the harvest was down to below 1.5 million tons, compared with over 4 million tons in 1899, but the *New York Times* pointed out that there were large stocks left, and there was plenty of ice up in Maine.

As reporters pursued their investigation of the price rise, they began to build up a picture of Morse's stranglehold on the city. By 1900, between a third and a quarter of New York's ice was manufactured, and the American Ice Company had tightened its grip on supplies by buying up some of the largest of the ice-manufacturing companies so they could not take advantage of the poor harvest. But it was clear to the *New York Times* that the American Ice Company was not simply a monopoly: it was in league with the New York Dock Department to drive out competition.

New York had a unique system for taking its ice deliveries. There were no large icehouses on the quays, as there were in Philadelphia or Baltimore. Because for years the ice had come down the Hudson on barges, these acted as ice stores, and ice was taken directly from them to be sold around town. To trade in ice, you therefore had to have a space to unload at the docks. There had been many disputes between the shipowners of Maine and the ice companies of New York over delays in unloading, as the schooners were treated as if they too were floating icehouses—their owners had sued for loss of ice after being kept waiting at the docks for days or weeks. Control of the docks was crucial to the ice trade, and it appeared that many companies had had difficulty in renewing their leases. Dock department workmen had demolished bridges and other essential buildings belonging to American Ice's rivals on the grounds that they were a nuisance, or unsafe. There was more than a whiff of corruption in the air, for city hall ran the docks, and there were demands for a full investigation into the activities of the ice trust, the monopolistic consortium of ice companies that attempted to give the appearance of competing concerns while they were, in fact, controlled by the president of American Ice, Charles Morse. In a long article in the May 6 issue, the *New York Times* noted a report in Boston newspapers that New York's Mayor Van Wyck had been seen at the Columbia Theatre with Morse. Mayor Van Wyck had refused to give an interview, commenting only that he was "on a pleasure trip" as Mr. Morse's guest.

Less than a month later, the books of the American Ice Company were handed anonymously to the *New York Journal*. They revealed that the mayor was a major shareholder, along with thirty other New York City officials, judges, and politicians. Morse was asked to testify before the Attorney General but chose instead to abandon the ice business altogether, taking a few million dollars with him. Some years later, he was involved in another scandal and was sent to jail, not for debt like Frederic Tudor, but for corrupt dealings.

The American Ice Company continued in business, drawing its supplies from both the natural-ice fields and artificial manufacturing. It was those in the food trade who first began to acquire their own refrigerators, but the problem of making a domestic model was not solved for many years, despite the evidence that if they could be made cheaply enough, there would be a huge demand for them in America.

The winter weather remained a subject of intense public concern in New York right up to the First World War. On February 2, 1906, the *New York Times* carried the headline: "ICE FAMINE THREATENS UNLESS COLD SETS IN—Twenty Days' Hard Frost Needed to Make a Crop—NONE HARVESTED ON HUDSON—New York Needs 4,000,000 Tons a Year and Artificial Plants Can Supply Only 700,000." The *Times* visited the American Ice Company to find out what was going on, and reported:

> The officers of the corporation were engaged in discussing the proper frame to buy for a twig of pussy willow in full bud . . . The twig bore a card on which was written "Plucked at Swan Island, Maine on Jan 31 1906." The plucking was done by the Maine superintendent of the company and the twig will be carefully preserved as a reminder of the conditions with which the ice business is confronted this year.

There was no ice at all on the Hudson, and artificial-ice plants that usually operated only in summer were being put to work to do what they could to make up the shortfall. The ice harvesters were out of work, and the only hope was for a freeze that would produce ice thick enough to get the horses out. The American Ice Company reckoned it could put together a workforce of ten thousand, who could harvest two hundred thousand tons a day if the weather hardened. In the end, Maine came to the rescue once again, but the price of ice rose.

The following year, 1907, a report by Dr. Daniel D. Jackson, a chemist working in New York's Department of Water Supply, Gas and Electricity, declared Hudson River ice unsafe to put into drinks. Twenty-five samples of ice had been taken from a 150-mile stretch of the Hudson where harvesting took place and had been brought in sealed jars to the department's laboratory. Most of the samples, Dr. Jackson reported, contained "intestinal germs," though he was unable to say what they were exactly. The samples were analyzed for smell, which ranged from "none" through "vegetable" and "disagreeable" to "rank." Some of the ice was judged "good," but at least half the samples were contaminated with something or other. The great fear was that it contained the bacteria that causes typhoid, and Dr. Jackson recommended stricter regulation of the ice trade, and a ban on the use of Hudson ice except for refrigeration. The then president of the American Ice Company, a Mr. Oler, rejected the report out of hand, arguing that the top of the ice, where most pollution would accumulate, was planed off before the ice was harvested, and that typhoid germs could not remain alive in ice for more than a few weeks, while the Hudson River crop was sold much longer than that after it was cut. Medical opinion was divided, but in the end the ice was declared reasonably safe.

By now the pressure of public opinion, however, was to end the city's reliance on natural ice: the supply was unreliable, it was increasingly dirty, and the delivery system that had seemed a wonder when it began back in the mid-nineteenth century was extremely inconvenient. The ice deliverymen were regarded as rough and unpleasant, and messed the house up with their wet boots. A number of newspaper articles suggested that Americans should give up their ice addiction because it was ruining their health, and that food stored in ice was unpalatable.

There was no going back. More and more ice-manufacturing plants were built, and by the outbreak of the First World War, the natural-ice industry was on the verge of collapse. Fires regularly destroyed the timber icehouses, which were kept as dry as possible and were therefore highly flammable despite their freezing contents. Sparks from the boilers that produced the steam for the conveyor belts, or from trains that ran near the sheds, were often responsible. There was a series of fires on the Kennebec River in the early 1900s; some suspected they were deliberately started to limit the supply and maintain prices, though, generally, most of the huge stacks of ice could survive a fire and still be sold.

On June 29, 1910, a disastrous fire began in a stable on the Kennebec; a spark from a train was the most likely cause. A high wind fanned the flames, and burning shingles set fire to icehouses belonging to the American Ice Company at Iceboro, from which the flames leaped to two schooners on the river. One of them, the *Henry L. Peckham,* was almost fully loaded, but she was aground on the low tide and could not be moved. The other, the *Young Brothers,* was on open water, but her anchor was caught and she could not get away. Both ships were destroyed, as were the icehouses and forty thousand tons of ice. The total losses amounted to $130,000. As one historian of the Kennebec trade put it, this was a "spectacular Viking funeral" for the Maine ice industry, which never recovered its former glory.

The industry that Frederic Tudor had begun in 1806 had created a demand for ice in America that had to be satisfied. In the long run, it was clear that scientists and technologists would be obliged to invent a convenient refrigerator for the home. The year before the Iceboro ice sheds were burned down, a French Cistercian monk and physics teacher, Marcel Audiffren, had demonstrated to a fascinated gathering at a congress in Paris his invention of an electrically driven, sealed-container refrigerator that used sulfur dioxide gas. He had been working on it for some time, and had had it patented in a number of countries in 1895. Working models were made in France in 1903 and in the United States in 1904. This was the prototype of the modern household refrigerator.

Whereas the steam-driven refrigerators used by ice-manufacturing companies were bulky, and required the constant presence of an operator to control the pressure and keep everything working smoothly, the Audiffren model was self-regulating. Many other inventions that sought to achieve the same result in different ways were patented, but all of them were hampered by the difficulty of making miniature compressors. The crucial development of small electric motors advanced rapidly during and just after the First World War, and a very-much-refined version of Audiffren's refrigerator was finally produced by the American company General Electric. In 1926, two thousand were sold. By 1931, there were a million models of various designs made, and in 1937 nearly three million. Just as Frederic Tudor's endeavors had made the United States the first nation in history to regard refrigeration as a necessity of life, America would also lead the way in the ownership of domestic coolers, as the gleaming new piece of kitchen equipment replaced the messy and inconvenient daily delivery of the summer ice to which Americans had been long accustomed. By 1950, 90 percent of Americans living in towns and 80 percent living in rural areas owned domestic refrigerators. In Britain and Europe, the domestic demand for ice had never become established, and it was not until after the Second World War that the American habit of putting ice in drinks and preserving food at home in refrigerators caught on.

The harvesting of ice did not disappear altogether. Remote rural areas in the northern United States that were late in getting an electricity supply continued to cut winter ice for their iceboxes into the 1940s and 1950s. But finally, a century and a half after its first faltering beginnings as Frederic Tudor's "slippery speculation," the frozen-water trade would come to an end. It had brought the first ice cream to the West Indies, supplied the British in India with ice for half a century, kept America's southern states cool the year round, and established refrigeration as a necessity of modern life, both for the preservation of food and as a home comfort. In the industry's heyday, harvested ice had been vital for all the great cities of North America, and supplying them required a winter workforce that must have numbered in the hundreds of thousands of men. Tens of thousands of horses were harnessed to plows and wagons, and along the East Coast, hundreds of ships and barges were employed in the trade. All of this huge industry simply melted away when artificial refrigeration finally offered a cheaper and more efficient way of making ice and creating cold, and the heroic labors of the ice harvesters were forgotten.

Epilogue

When I was researching this book, I spent some time at the Baker Library at Harvard Business School, which holds the largest collection of Frederic Tudor's papers, including the icehouse diaries. Harvard is close to Fresh Pond, and I planned to make a pilgrimage there, hoping to see it frozen. I was a bit late in the year, for it was already early March, and the temperature had risen to the seventies. Students were eating their lunch on the lawns and Rollerblading about the campus in T-shirts.

I turned on the Weather Channel that evening, and was astonished to learn that snow was forecast for the following morning. Sure enough, there was a bitter wind and driving snow when I looked out of the window the next day, and the lawns at Harvard on which students had picnicked the day before were a glistening white. The following day it was still bitterly cold, with a thin layer of snow on the ground and a clear sky: good ice-making weather. So with a friend I made my pilgrimage to Fresh Pond. I was very excited, and wondered what kind of memorial there would be to commemorate the fact that ice had once been cut here and sent as far away as India. I had a map that showed a small "Tudor Park" on the shoreline.

We walked all the way around Fresh Pond, but found no sign of Tudor Park, nor any plaque, monument, or mention of Frederic Tudor and the ice trade at all. There was not even much ice: just a few bits clinging to the vegetation that poked up through the clear water. Fresh Pond has for many years been an important reservoir for the Cambridge water supply, and it is fenced off to prevent pollution. A new water-treatment plant was being built on the shore. The only relic of the ice trade is the railway line. There is not a trace of an ice-house, though there must be a few ice-harvesting tools lying on the bottom of the pond. This historic stretch of water is now part of sub-urban Cambridge, which comes to shop at the nearby Fresh Pond Mall.

On the day I visited, a few well-muffled joggers and strollers out with their dogs were circumnavigating the pond. As I had been surprised and disappointed to find no memorial to Frederic Tudor or the ice trade, I thought I would ask one or two locals if they had any idea of the immense significance of the pond and the shoreline on which they were strolling. Nobody had heard of the Boston Ice King, and when I mentioned that ice from Fresh Pond had been sold in India more than a century before, I could see a shadow of doubt fall across the faces of those I stopped. "Is this guy crazy?" I sensed they were asking themselves. "How could you sell ice to India without a refrigerator?" What had been considered absurd in 1806, when Frederic began the frozen-water trade sounds, if any-thing, even more ridiculous today. Which is perhaps why this whole extraordinary episode in American history has been almost completely forgotten, even in the town in which it originated. And who now could believe that in 1906 a great city like New York was thrown into a panic because the winter up in Maine had been warm enough for a pussy willow to bloom in January? It may sound crazy—but it's true.

Index

9 780786 886401